Praise for *Trust Your Vibes*

"Trust your vibes and read this book! The straightforward, practical advice (backed up with solid examples of how well it works) will show you how to use your most valuable asset—your sixth sense."
— **Cheryl Richardson,** the *New York Times* best-selling author of *Take Time for Your Life* and *Life Makeovers*

"With every word, Sonia's gift to simplify the seemingly complex and arcane 'hidden world' of inner wisdom brings truth closer to the heart. Trust her vibes!"
— **Billy Corgan,** singer, songwriter, and founder of the Smashing Pumpkins and Zwan

"For more than 14 years, Sonia Choquette has been a trusted advisor and tour guide of my life. Her vision gives me confidence in myself and what lies in store for me. When Sonia shares her amazing gifts with you, doors you've never seen before start to open right before your very eyes."
— **Wendy Miller,** Emmy Award–winning producer and writer

"Sonia has had a huge impact on our business by helping us to utilize our intuition as a critical building tool. Any company in the 21st century needs to embrace the sixth sense, and Sonia is a wise, dynamic teacher who helps us to 'trust our vibes,' even when others might disagree with the direction. We've loved the results!"
— **Scott and Kim Holstein,** Kim and Scott's Gourmet Pretzels

*"Sonia's grace and wisdom surpass her extremely gifted psychic abilities, and help us remember the psychic being that lives within each one of us. Her book **Trust Your Vibes** is a divine example of this, as she openly shares ways for us to connect with our intuition and enhance our lives. It is truly a gift!"*
— **James Twyman,** the author of *Emissary of Love*

"Sonia's path is one of self-discovery, of spirit wed to heart and logic."
— **Charlotte Beers,** advertising CEO

TRUST YOUR VIBES

Also by Sonia Choquette

*Diary of a Psychic**

The Psychic Pathway

The Psychic Pathway to New Beginnings

The Psychic Pathway to Joy

True Balance

Trust Your Vibes Oracle Card Deck (available August 2004)*

The Wise Child

Your Heart's Desire

---

*Also published by Hay House

Please visit Hay House USA: **www.hayhouse.com**
Hay House Australia: **www.hayhouse.com.au**
Hay House UK: **www.hayhouse.co.uk**
Hay House South Africa: **orders@psdprom.co.za**

TRUST YOUR VIBES

Secret Tools for Six-Sensory Living

Sonia Choquette

HAY HOUSE, INC.
Carlsbad, California
London • Sydney • Johannesburg
Vancouver • Hong Kong

Published and distributed in the United States by: Hay House, Inc., P.O. Box 5100, Carlsbad, CA 92018-5100 • *Phone:* (760) 431-7695 or (800) 654-5126 • *Fax:* (760) 431-6948 or (800) 650-5115 • www.hayhouse.com • **Published and distributed in Australia by:** Hay House Australia, Ltd., 18/36 Ralph St., Alexandria NSW 2015 • *Phone:* 612-9669-4299 • *Fax:* 612-9669-4144 • www.hayhouse.com.au • **Published and distributed in the United Kingdom by:** Hay House UK, Ltd. • Unit 62, Canalot Studios • 222 Kensal Rd., London W10 5BN • *Phone:* 44-20-8962-1230 • *Fax:* 44-20-8962-1239 • www.hayhouse.co.uk • **Published and distributed in the Republic of South Africa by:** Hay House SA (Pty), Ltd., P.O. Box 990, Witkoppen 2068 • *Phone/Fax:* 2711-7012233 • orders@psdprom.co.za • **Distributed in Canada by:** Raincoast • 9050 Shaughnessy St., Vancouver, B.C. V6P 6E5 • *Phone:* (604) 323-7100 • *Fax:* (604) 323-2600

Editorial supervision: Jill Kramer
Design: Summer McStravick

Library of Congress Cataloging-in-Publication Data

Choquette, Sonia.
  Trust your vibes : secret tools for six-sensory living / Sonia Choquette.
       p. cm.
  ISBN 1-40190-232-4 (hardcover) — ISBN 1-40190-233-2 (tradepaper)
  1. Intuition. I. Title.
  BF315.5 .C47 2004
  133.8—dc21

2002152857

Hardcover ISBN 1-4019-0232-4
Tradepaper ISBN 1-4019-0233-2

07 06 05 04   4 3 2 1
1st printing, March 2004

Printed in the United States of America

This book is dedicated to my daughters,
Sonia and Sabrina. Thank you for the gift of your
delightful spirits; your wise insights; your endless sense
of humor; your honesty; and your profoundly generous,
forgiving, and loving hearts. It is my greatest joy to be
your mother and to witness your souls as they
emerge into the world. You are my light.

And to my mother, who taught me to trust
my vibes, no matter what. I shall be forever
grateful for the gifts you have given me.

CONTENTS

———◇ ◇ ◇———

Author's Note: *Every story in this book is true, but most names have been changed to protect the privacy of those concerned.*

———◇ ◇ ◇———

INTRODUCTION

As a professional intuitive and spiritual teacher who's been practicing for more than 32 years, I've spent most of my life helping people realize on an intuitive level that we're all spiritual beings endowed with *six*, not five, senses. What's even more important is that we *need* that sixth sense to fulfill our life's purpose and to be peaceful and happy.

My mission began as a child in Denver, Colorado, when I started doing one-on-one intuitive readings at the age of 12 for people at my kitchen table. More formal training in the six-sensory arts followed when I began apprenticing for many years with my two spiritual and intuitive master teachers, Charlie Goodman and Dr. Trenton Tully. In addition to this private, specialized teaching, I spent 25 years studying the areas of religion, language, and mysticism (including Western kabbalah and other world religions, Western mysticism, and tarot) to help me better understand the soul's evolution.

But the best education I've had has come from the intuitive readings themselves, which I've done for clients on almost a daily basis since I was 12. Working in the trenches with each person has given me more insight than any formal classroom could have ever offered. The opportunity to study and witness my clients' evolution has been an extraordinary education in just how essential our sixth sense—or our "vibes," as I like to call them—is to successful living. So, throughout this book, I'll tell real-life stories of how my clients learned to tap in to their sixth sense and really start to trust their vibes, and I'll demonstrate how this changed and improved their lives.

Through all my training and experience, I've come to fully understand what I refer to as our "throwaway" sense and how we can call it back into our lives. Our sixth or psychic sense is not a *physical* sense like the other five—it's more of a *spiritual* sense, which is connected to our soul body and centered in the heart. Just as our physical senses keep our body informed and directed, our sixth sense's primary function is to guide our soul's growth and keep us connected to our Creator, our spirit guides, and our angelic assistants, who direct us in our path and purpose.

Our physical senses give us our feet and keep us earthbound, while our sixth sense gives us our wings and teaches us to soar. Sadly, few people realize that we have such an important spiritual sense, let alone know how to access or listen to it.

As time moves on and the world becomes more complicated, my mission as a six-sensory guide and teacher has become more urgent. I believe that recognizing we have vibes and giving them a proper place in our world is no longer optional if we hope to live meaningful, secure, and balanced lives. We must stop questioning or resisting our higher wisdom and accept the now scientifically supported reality that we are, indeed, far more conscious and capable on a soul level than we've been taught to believe or have dared to express. We must learn to trust our vibes—those energetic bursts rising out of our inborn psychic sense that pulse subtly through our awareness and guide us through our soul's journey.

The price people pay for ignoring their vibes is high: They end up living in fear, feeling inadequate and powerless. They make decisions that aren't good for them, which leads them to places other than where they want to be. They become anxious and addictive, acting aggressively, even violently, toward those they love, thus alienating themselves even more. They become stressed, even physically ill, and enjoy no real peace of mind. Wandering around in the darkness of second-guessing and worry, they fight against life or get trampled beneath it and fail to achieve their purpose or spiritual goals, thus wasting, instead of loving, their lives.

I know this because after all these years of reading for people, I've observed it firsthand many times. All confusion and stress is unnecessary: It's not our design, it's impractical, and it isn't in the Divine order to feel so lost or vulnerable.

As a practicing six-sensory guide, I can assure you that listening to your vibes cures this fear and stress. It will establish a direct link to your Creator and your spirit guides and helpers. It will guide you safely to your path, connect you to the right relationships, assist you in learning your spiritual secrets, guide you in your profession, keep you safe and out of harm's way, and help you realize that you're loved and accepted just as you are. Your sixth sense supports your creativity, helps heal your emotional wounds, and calms your anxious and uncertain heart. Through direction from your angels, guides, and Higher Self, your vibes bring you peace of mind and show you how to live a higher, more harmonious way.

My sixth sense has always been my greatest gift. It has cut away the confusion and illusions that once left me feeling isolated and alone, and it has made me aware of how we're all in this experience called life together.

Those of us who trust our vibes have several things in common: We listen to our helpers, spirit guides, and angels—those light beings devoted to our growth and healing, who show us our proper place in the Universal scheme of things. We pay attention to and respect what we feel at all times, even if it doesn't make sense at the moment. We think, feel, and act on our vibes without question or hesitation, unlike those who aren't six-sensory—or, as I prefer, aren't *yet* six-sensory. As intuitive beings, we're as attuned to the unseen world as we are to the physical one (maybe more so).

It's almost as though six-sensory and five-sensory people are two different species. Six-sensory people trust their vibes and let their psychic energy lead them day by day; and generally speaking, six-sensory people are more creative, resourceful, and successful than five-sensory people in every way. What I've observed most of all in my professional capacity is that psychic individuals enjoy life more fully than nonpsychic people do.

Having six senses brings with it an innate sense of security, confidence, and courage, which those stuck in a five-sensory paradigm fail to have. We know that our spirits live on after death, so we don't fight against the tides of life. We don't fear death and get caught in the undertow of mortal anxiety; instead, we surf the waves of life gracefully and with faith because we know that we have help behind the scenes and that we're eternal. Above all, people who trust their vibes realize that love is the magic potion that gives us our wings.

Another fundamental difference between "six-sensories" (that is, those who trust their vibes) and "five-sensories" (those who don't) is the rules they follow for life. Five-sensory people only see the physical plane and follow *intellectual* or *ego-based* laws, while six-sensory people feel the spiritual plane and follow *spiritual* law, thus creating two contrasting realities: the ordinary way and the higher way. A six-sensory being's vibration is faster, lighter, more attractive, more fluid and healing, and can be immediately felt. Others are drawn to this higher vibration because it feels so good.

This isn't to say that six-sensory people are superior to those who aren't—any developed six-sensory person will tell you that we're *all* Divine spiritual beings who come from the same source, have the same worth, and are made of the same essence: love. I only suggest that people who trust their vibes tend to have a superior life experience because they're better informed and can make better choices, which usually leads to a greater ability to love and appreciate this wonderful life.

Trust Your Vibes reveals the secrets to awakening your sixth sense. In it, I share practices, tools, and perspectives that we six-sensory people live by. People who trust their vibes pay attention to life differently—in attitude, perspective, and approach. We look for different clues, and are more sensitive and perceptive than those who have shut down or are unaware of their higher wisdom and guidance.

Most of all, six-sensory people take the bold step of going *with* their feelings instead of wasting time struggling *against* them, and we never concern ourselves with whether or not they make sense to others. We know that our sixth sense operates out of linear time and space and, therefore, will sometimes give us information that won't make immediate sense, but will eventually.

Of course, we don't know everything that will happen to us or to others in advance, but we do know that we'll be guided and shown the best possible direction for our growth, protection, and well-being. Consequently, we don't worry about the future. Six-sensory people base their habits, behaviors, and decisions on what they feel inside, rather than on what they're told outside; the result is that they feel at peace within themselves and in the Universe most of the time.

The good news is that we're all naturally designed to be six-sensory beings; that is, to be psychically guided to some degree depending on the overall evolution and intention of our soul. Some people (like me) are here to serve as guides and teachers to others as our soul mission, while others use their sixth sense on a more personal level. Yet we're all capable of being six-sensory when it comes to our own purpose and protection. When we disconnect from our internal guidance system, we become lost and disoriented. This isn't the natural way to live, nor is it necessary. Once you learn to activate your vibes, you can begin to eliminate all this confusion and start to be just as guided as I am.

My mission as a professional psychic has always been to serve as a teacher, to be the bridge that leads other people back to their inner psychic navigational system. This book is another expression of that mission. It's offered as an insider's look at the psychic life so that those who are ready to step into the Divine and live an easier, gentler, and more satisfying way of life can do so.

There *is* a way to open up to your psychic energy system and learn to trust your vibes. In this book, I'll share what we six-sensory people do, how we think, the choices we make, and the attitudes and perspectives we own. In modeling after six-sensory people, you, too, can activate your own vibes. As a teacher, I love nothing more than to guide people to open their psychic lives. But as a member of the human race, I feel it's urgent that people wake up their sixth sense, because without it, we're making no sense at all. We're hurting one another, killing in the name of God, drugging ourselves in epidemic proportions, and living in isolated states, while the world is overcrowding at record levels.

Six-sensory awareness heals all of the above because, at its root, it helps us see how we're all interconnected and inter-dependent, and therefore, "whatsoever we do to the least of our brothers [is what] indeed we do to ourselves." Following our vibes serves as a great deterrent to the downward spiral of personal and global self-destruction we find ourselves tangled in today. When we trust our vibes, we restore our balance and experience within—which, ultimately, leads to peace without.

}—◇ ◇ ◇—{

HOW TO USE THIS BOOK

My purpose in writing this book is to help you open your intuitive channels and to teach you how to trust your vibes. I'll do this by sharing the secret practices that professional six-sensory people use every day to navigate the unseen world of spirit. I want to help you shift your identity from being ego-based to being soul-based, to strengthen your intuitive muscles, and to build your psychic confidence. By using these practices, you'll anchor your sixth sense in a grounded and practical fashion.

I'll introduce these six-sensory secrets one at a time, in order to give you a sense of how to experience the world through an intuitive perspective, and then you'll try each one to see if it works for you. This approach will train you to think like a six-sensory being who experiences the world through your vibes instead of through your head, or intellect, as five-sensory people do.

The practices are graduated, starting with the basic need of preparing your body to feel subtle energy, and then organizing the rest of your awareness to tune in to higher psychic vibrations. The 33 practices are divided into 9 groups, or parts—keep in mind that each part builds on the one preceding it, as you move toward the realization of your sixth, psychic sense. In other words, much like a music-appreciation course, you'll first learn the notes of six-sensory living, then the melodies of your vibes, and finally, the composition of intuitive creativity and how we build our lives to support our soul's evolution.

In learning to live "vibrationally" from the foundation up, you'll gain experience in trusting your vibes one tiny step at a time. Read each secret at your own pace, and then follow with the suggested practice for a few days and see what happens. Each secret builds on the one before, gently providing a platform on which to develop your personal six-sensory experiences easily and comfortably. Some secrets you may already know and practice, while others may be completely new to you. Be open-minded and give each one a try, setting your own course. In this way, you'll learn to trust your vibes no matter what you're facing.

Look at this book as a gentle workout program for exercising your psychic muscles, and think of me as your personal trainer; after all, as a professional intuitive who's worked with thousands of people and has observed how they learn, I know what works and what doesn't, as well as where the traps are. Small steps work—grandiose goals don't.

When you trust your vibes, you change the rules that run your life and can then begin to take the risk of following your spirit, thereby enhancing your own intuitive abilities. Even though we all have the potential to be six-sensory beings and can be guided by our Higher Self, wanting to be is not enough. In the same way that watching an exercise video won't give you abs of steel, neither will knowing about your intuition or just wanting to be intuitive make you intuitive. Unless you *train* your psychic muscles and use them daily, they won't develop into the strong inner vibrational-guidance system that's intended.

It may feel awkward to practice the secrets in this book at first, but if you stick with them, that will change. Leaving the head and moving into the heart takes time and some getting used to. It won't take an inordinate amount of time do so, and if you approach this process lightly and with fun, instead of making it a test, you'll be communicating with the Universe like a six-sensory pro in no time. Soon you'll stop looking outside yourself for answers. You'll know in your heart what's right for you because you'll feel your vibes and hear your Higher Self loud and clear.

As spiritual beings, we all have psychic wings and want to fly with our souls. We want to rise above life's struggles and live a higher way because we intuitively know in our bones that we can. The way to fly with spirit is simple, so stop fighting and start listening to it. It *will* lift you up.

I believe we all know on some level that "something is wrong with this picture" when we don't trust our vibes or when we ignore our spirit. If you want to move away from fear and retrieve the missing link in your awareness and are ready to make the commitment to do so, you can. If you want to follow your spirit, hear your spirit guides, and see beyond appearances and into a deeper understanding of yourself and others, you can. If you want to be in touch with loved ones who have crossed over, contact angelic forces, and tap in to geniuses from past eras, you can do this, too.

In my first book, *The Psychic Pathway*, I introduced you to your sixth sense. In this book, I'll show you how to develop this sense into the powerful guidance system it's intended to be. If your desire to trust your vibes and live a psychically guided life matches my desire to teach you how, then together we're going to succeed.

)—◇ ◇ ◇—(

QUIZ

ARE YOU A SIX-SENSORY BEING?

B efore you begin reading about the tools and secrets I have regarding living a six-sensory life, it might be helpful to recognize how attuned you are to your vibes. Complete the following questionnaire, checking one choice after each statement.

		Rarely	**Sometimes**	**Often**
1.	When I'm with someone, I easily understand how they feel.	_____	_____	_____
2.	I love to physically move and exercise.	_____	_____	_____
3.	I listen to my gut feelings, even if they don't make sense.	_____	_____	_____
4.	I'm aware of when someone is lying to me or manipulating me.	_____	_____	_____
5.	I can tell if I'm on the wrong track, and I change it.	_____	_____	_____
6.	I know when someone is misleading me.	_____	_____	_____
7.	I tend to get overly involved with other people's problems.	_____	_____	_____
8.	I get immediate answers even when I don't fully understand the problem.	_____	_____	_____

	Rarely	**Sometimes**	**Often**
9. I change my plans easily if I get bad vibes.	_____	_____	_____
10. I share what I have and don't worry about having enough.	_____	_____	_____
11. I feel protected in some way, as though someone is watching over me.	_____	_____	_____
12. I can say no even when it's difficult.	_____	_____	_____
13. I express my true feelings, even when they're unpopular.	_____	_____	_____
14. I trust myself to make the final decision.	_____	_____	_____
15. I'm careful whom I ask for advice.	_____	_____	_____
16. I like to take risks and try new things.	_____	_____	_____
17. I take care of my body.	_____	_____	_____
18. I pay attention to people and listen closely when they speak.	_____	_____	_____
19. I know things before they happen.	_____	_____	_____
20. I often think of people, and then they call me the same day.	_____	_____	_____
21. I sense whether people and situations are good for me or not.	_____	_____	_____
22. I'm a creative thinker and love to doodle or play when I have a free moment.	_____	_____	_____
23. I have a great sense of humor.	_____	_____	_____
24. There are a lot of coincidences in my life.	_____	_____	_____
25. I believe I have helpers on the Other Side, such as guardian angels.	_____	_____	_____

When you've completed the questionnaire, go back and look at your answers. Give yourself one point for each "Rarely," two points for each "Sometimes," and three points for each "Often."

- **If your score was 25–39:**
  You're not presently in the habit of noticing your sixth sense—but this will change rapidly when you use the tools and secrets in this book. As you open to your intuitive self, your sense of adventure and vitality will increase significantly.

- **If your score was 40–59:**
  You're already quite tuned in to your sixth sense, although you may not call it that. You may just consider yourself "hypersensitive" or "lucky." As you work with these secret six-sensory tools, you'll experience an increasing sense of safety, guidance, and creativity, and your life will become much more exciting and satisfying.

- **If your score was 60–75:**
  You probably realize that your sixth sense is exceptionally developed, but you may not trust it completely. As you practice the tools in this book, you'll develop the confidence you need to begin living the joyful life of a fully awakened six-sensory being. You'll learn how to navigate through life with grace and ease, and soar above problems rather than struggle through them. You'll awaken your spirit and learn to fly.

So, now that you know you're ready to become a six-sensory being and start trusting your vibes, let's begin.

PART I

Begin with the Basics

SECRET #1

"WOO-WOO" IS WHERE IT'S AT

I f you want to trust your vibes, you must absolutely "get" that you have a psychic sixth sense that picks them up, even if it's dormant right now. Your sixth sense is your natural inner genius, and even though you might not believe in it, it's normal to be a spiritual being guided by the Universe. Six-sensory, psychic people know this; nonpsychic, five-sensory people don't. So, if you want to live a higher way, stop doubting when your intuition speaks to you, stop ignoring your sixth sense when you feel it, and start accepting and appreciating your vibes when they do activate.

First, you must change your attitude. You can't go along with five-sensory types who think that six-sensory people are crazy or just plain weird. You simply can't lock the sixth sense out of your life. Even Leonardo da Vinci, one of my all-time favorite six-sensory people, was considered a nut and a heretic by his five-sensory associates— as were Thomas Edison and Walt Disney, among others. Of course, the world has reconsidered, and now recognizes these men as great creative, intuitive geniuses, but five-sensory people still regularly discount the sixth sense because their egos will do anything to stay in control. But instead of worrying that you'll look like an oddball if you let on that you have vibes, be happy about it. This means that you're progressing beyond the five-sensory norm.

Second, in order to have a six-sensory life, you must come up with reasons to listen to your intuition. Intuitives like me know that listening to your vibes is practical, saves time, connects the dots of your life, and even improves relationships. Best of all, trusting your vibes relieves you of worry—that alone should be enough of an incentive to get your sixth sense up and running.

For example, my student Bea and her husband recently decided to sell their big home in Dayton, Ohio, and move to a smaller town house nearby. The couple's children were grown, so they wanted a place that would afford them more freedom and less expense. "The only thing I don't look forward to," Bea told me, "is having to show my house to strangers. I wish I could just sell it without any hassle or intrusion."

Heeding my advice and following my psychic example in how to be six-sensory, Bea turned the problem over to her guides and put it out of her mind. Now, she wasn't one to discuss her private life openly, but the next morning, Bea felt inclined to tell her new cleaning lady, Lori, about her plans. So, when Lori arrived, Bea trusted her vibes and confided that she and her husband were thinking about selling the house.

"Oh my God!" Lori exclaimed. "I can't believe you said that! Another client of mine asked me just yesterday to help her find a house in this neighborhood. Knowing her taste, I bet she'd *love* this place."

The timing was perfect. Lori put the two women in touch that day, and it was a match—in fact, the house was practically sold over the phone. By being a good six-sensory student, and trusting her vibes instead of struggling with them, Bea attracted a solution for her problem in less than a day.

Delighted, but not the least bit surprised, Bea watched how Lori, a five-sensory person, couldn't get over what had happened. Such psychic efficiency confused Lori because she was used to life being much more complicated. She reacted by remarking, "It's almost creepy how this all worked out!"

Bea saw nothing creepy about it at all, for she expected nothing less than the synchronistic unfolding that occurred. After all, that's how our sixth sense works. All Bea said about it was, "Thank you." And that day she graduated fully into six-sensory living.

Another student of mine, a shy and somewhat introverted 46-year-old engineer named Raymond, was just beginning to open up his intuition, and he couldn't quite believe that it could actually show up and help him. For months he joked with his friends about how he'd like to avoid the dating scene that he loathed, saying, "I'd just like to push a button and make my dream gal appear."

One day as he was heading to a business meeting at a local hotel, Raymond pushed the elevator's button. The doors opened to reveal the most attractive woman Raymond had ever seen—and she was going to the same meeting. To his surprise, the attraction was mutual. Raymond's vibes, in search of his heart's desire, navigated him (as it naturally does) to intercept her, but his mind struggled with the outcome. Reverting back to his old five-sensory rules, Raymond worried that his dream girl would go away just as strangely as she appeared. She didn't, and they're now engaged to be married. He's learning. . . .

The good news is that today, as we march firmly into the New Age and science recognizes that the sixth sense is real, it's much more modern and intelligent to get with it and learn to trust your vibes as natural gifts, rather than seeing them as alien.

What science and spiritual law now agree on is that each and every one of us is a six-sensory creature, and everything in the Universe is interconnected. We psychically influence each other at all times, and those of us who live in a higher way know this as fact and don't question it. Because of this interconnection, it makes sense that Raymond's void attracted the right partner in his girlfriend, and that Bea's desire to effortlessly sell her house attracted the perfect buyer.

Synchronicities are not flukes or random events—they're intentional reflections of our intuition working with the perfect order of all things in the unseen world. It's why fish swim upstream, birds fly south, and bears hibernate. Everything in nature intuitively gravitates toward what best serves its growth, and that includes the human race. The only difference is that we have the choice to follow our intuition or not. So if you want your sixth sense to work, stop resisting your vibes, and change the rules you live by instead. As one intuitive friend of mine said to her very modern 85-year-old Jungian therapist, "I'm just afraid that I'll seem too 'woo-woo' to my friends." To which the therapist replied, "But my dear, don't you realize that 'woo-woo' is where it's at these days?"

I agree. I can't imagine life without my vibes leading the way. I'm so accustomed to listening for inner guidance that I wouldn't know how to direct myself without it. It would be like being blindfolded on a gorgeous day—why would I want to miss the beauty around me? Those who are disconnected from their sixth sense are handicapped, and unnecessarily so. Why would you purposely ignore a compass and map and wander in the dark?

I have a confession to make: The reasons for my campaigning here aren't entirely selfless. Have you ever been on a highway when some fool enters and drives in the wrong direction, goes well below the speed limit, or changes lanes sporadically because he's afraid or doesn't know where he's going? It creates chaos and annoyingly throws everyone else out of sync. The same thing happens to a six-sensory person like me living in a world filled with five-sensory control freaks who are afraid to get in the flow. It breaks my stride, bogs me down, and can be really irritating. So my roadster self is definitely invested in getting everyone up to speed so that I can travel the psychic highway without running into energy roadblocks or traffic jams.

I know this sounds selfish, but in truth, it isn't. It feels great to get into the flow of life and go where I really want to be, and I just want everyone else to join me there. If we are to evolve as a race and live together on this planet in any semblance of harmony, we need to overcome the fear that comes from following five-sensory rules. The only way to make this happen is to embrace spiritual law and connect lovingly to each other by using our sixth sense. Throwing away the very tool we need to do this leaves us in the Dark Ages.

You can continue to be held hostage by following five-sensory laws and questioning or doubting your sixth sense, but sooner or later you'll realize that the six-sensory train to the future is going to great places, and you may be left standing at the station. Don't worry if you're afraid; it's normal when you enter the unknown. You can be afraid and still evolve. It's not *feeling* fear that stops you—after all, everyone feels fear at times— it's *hiding* your fear that gets in the way. That concealment takes all of your energy and leaves none for enjoying your life. So make friends with your fear, and then go for it!

Six-Sensory Practice

Get started on your path to higher living by accepting the fact that you're indeed *naturally intuitive,* even if your sixth sense isn't up and running to its full potential just yet. You can be a six-sensory beginner and still advance if you believe that it's possible, but you can't progress if you continue to argue with yourself about it. You must consider every feeling, thought, hit, hunch, aha!, bright idea, and "I wonder . . ." you experience as important expressions of your sixth sense. They're the lifelines of your vibes.

Think like a six-sensory person. Are you comfortable with your vibes? Are you in the habit of accepting them (which is spiritual law), or do you dismiss them as unworthy information (which is ego law)? Practice having a positive, matter-of-fact attitude toward your sixth sense, even if it doesn't feel natural yet. Pretend if you must—surprisingly, this works. And keep in mind that it will get easier. You're just beginning to train your awareness to follow a higher way, so it won't necessarily feel like "you" immediately.

To get out of your own way and on to your vibes even quicker, take a sheet of paper and write down all your fears, negative beliefs, or attitudes as they arise, whether they're from your own experiences or you've inherited them from other people. What ancient notions roll around in your brain and keep you from using your psychic genius? Keeping notes will make you aware of beliefs that you didn't even know you had.

As you look at your list, ask yourself if you really believe the old rules, or if they're just old habits. Are you ready to take a risk and change your attitude? If the answer is yes, then do so. That's the first step. You don't have to be a walking billboard to live a higher way, so don't get scared. Within these pages, I'll teach you how to implement your decision to change into your life, but you must decide once and for all that this is what you really want to do.

Next, practice your newly adopted attitude. Be aware of the subtle, intricate interconnections we all share, and appreciate them. Note the attitudes of those around you as well. How do others frame their intuitive and psychic experiences? Are they five- or six-sensory individuals? Understanding this distinction will make you far less defensive about your own vibes. If someone suggests that intuition or vibes are weird, how do you respond? Do you agree to avoid any unpleasantness, or do you speak up?

Every time you slip into old patterns, just say "Oh, well," and get back on track. And every time you choose the new attitude, following spiritual law over fear and control, give yourself a big hand. I mean it. You must become your greatest cheerleader on the adventure to six-sensory living, starting right now.

SIX-SENSORY WISDOM:

It's great to be six-sensory!

SECRET #2

THE SIXTH SENSE IS COMMON SENSE

First and foremost, you need to know that your sixth sense is founded on awareness. And in order to be aware of your vibes and learn to trust them, you must start with common sense. If you want your awareness to function on high, you must give your body what it needs so that it can be aware.

We human beings are exhausted these days, and not getting enough rest is death to our vibes. When you look up *intuition* in the dictionary, you'll notice that one definition is "to notice" and another is "to pay attention." When you're so sleep deprived that it's difficult to focus on what's right in front of your nose, chances are you won't notice much on the more subtle psychic plane of energy either. When you get this tired, your ego becomes a slave driver and doesn't feel—it only thinks. It can't feel when you're tired, so it will try to convince you that you aren't. *Don't listen to it.* And remember that when you sleep, your ego sleeps, too, thus freeing your intuitive voice.

One of the most practical suggestions for activating your sixth sense is to "sleep on it" when looking for guidance. My teacher Charlie Goodman once explained to me that sleep allows the emotions to rest and the spirit to wake up. For example, several years ago I found myself struggling over whether or not I should keep a particular babysitter I'd hired. Even though it seemed as if she was doing a good job of watching my daughters, my vibes told me that there was something terribly off about her—yet I couldn't put my finger on what it was. Since getting rid of her would have been very inconvenient, I wrestled with my uneasiness until I was worn out. Knowing what I do about exhaustion, I decided to sleep on it for one night and review it in the morning.

In my dream state, I saw my babysitter running frantically in circles, hiding her face and not paying attention to my kids or me as I tried to discuss the day with her. That was enough for me— I no longer struggled over my decision. For reasons I didn't understand (or need to), my psychic vibes told me that she had to go.

Relieved to have made a decision, I planned to let her go when she arrived that morning at ten. At nine I got a call from a man who identified himself as the babysitter's father. He asked if I knew his daughter; when I said that I did, he went on to tell me that she'd run away from home five months earlier. That explained my psychic wariness. Even though this girl was perfectly delightful, she was on the lam and needed to go home and clear up her life, which was obviously catching up with her. The funny thing was that she must have had a vibe, too, because she didn't show up that morning, or ever again. I guess we were both guided to do what we needed, and all it took for me to get it was a good night's sleep.

Getting enough rest is only part of the equation, however. You must also eat properly if you want to feel your vibes. You can't eat just anything and expect to be psychically aware— you've got to pay attention to what foods feed your body appropriately so that you don't keel over or shut down. As obvious as this is, I can't believe the amount of resistance most people have when it comes to following a reasonably healthy diet. Most people are either starving themselves to death or are subsisting on a diet of poorly chosen foods. Not surprisingly, they're usually exhausted, which, needless to say, doesn't leave much room for noticing your vibes.

It's unnecessary to follow a restricted or unusual diet to live in a higher way; instead, simply make sure that what you eat is good for you. Sugary doughnuts, dozens of cups of coffee, fast

food, and frozen dinners won't do the trick. You need to eat
nutritious food that supports your physical body. For instance, I
can't do proper psychic readings if I have too much sugar in the
morning and not enough protein. I need a lot of energy to focus,
and an insubstantial breakfast doesn't give it to me. So, on the
days I work, I have oatmeal to help me concentrate. This simple
change has made all the difference in the world.

You don't have to take my word for it or use your sixth sense
on this one—simply pay attention to how you feel when you eat.
If you make the connection between good food and good feelings, you'll see that it's fairly obvious. It isn't necessary to become
a vegetarian or exclusively eat sprouts and tofu; instead, just
make certain that your diet contains some life force, or is as close
to the natural source as possible. In other words, eat a healthy,
common-sense diet consisting of fruits, vegetables, adequate protein, and whole grains, and avoid packaged or processed foods.
Of course this isn't difficult to figure out, but it *does* challenge
ego rules, so it can be tricky.

Here's an example of what I mean. My client Constance was
a hardworking office administrator for an advertising agency.
She spent most days working from seven in the morning until
midnight, and she rarely ate a decent thing all week. She drank
way too much coffee; and her diet consisted of doughnuts, take-
out hamburgers, and restaurant meals. However, Constance's ego
told her that she shouldn't take even a few minutes to get something more sustaining or she'd miss something at work. No wonder she became burned-out and depressed, even though she loved
her job. Her diet was not only annihilating her vibes, it was dec-
imating her emotions and body.

When Constance came in for an intuitive reading, she said
that she'd asked her doctor for medication to alleviate her depression, but he didn't feel ready to give it to her. In my reading, I
suggested that instead of medication, she should simply change
her diet and see what happened. Yet she ignored my advice and
convinced her doctor to prescribe medication. The side effects
were so severe that she ended up coming back to me for help.
Again I insisted that a few good meals a week would make a

huge difference. This time she listened. She prepared her lunches at home and cooked her dinners after work despite being worn out. She began eating vegetables, gave up sugar, and ate more whole grains.

In just one month, Constance's depression lifted and her energy rebounded, as did her intuition. She became so inspired that she came up with some extremely imaginative campaigns for the agency and consequently won a promotion to the creative staff. Because of its mission to make right connections, it made sense that her intuition led her to success.

The ego never sees these hidden connections, while intuition sees them all the time. To this day, Constance rightly attributes her progress and inspiration to her homemade vegetable soup and her herbal tea and vitamins. I'm not suggesting that food should replace medication—after all, medication is a godsend to those who need it—however, medication doesn't replace real food. No matter how you look at it, we *all* need to eat properly to function at our best.

The Importance of Doing Nothing

To access your vibes, you must also give yourself more downtime. Besides refreshing your body, doing nothing affords you the inner space you need to refuel your psychic engines and perceive the subtle voice of spirit. While your fearful ego will urge you to keep going no matter what, your spirit knows that you should rest and let the Universe take over for a while. My friend Bill learned this lesson firsthand a few years ago.

Bill and his girlfriend were on vacation in Paris. One day, they decided to go their separate ways early in the morning and then meet back at a café next door to their hotel at five. Since they were staying in a small, quaint inn with an unusual room key, Bill said that he'd carry it. His girlfriend insisted that she'd be more responsible with the key, but Bill won. So their rendezvous was set.

After sightseeing and shopping, Bill headed for the café, exhausted and ready for a nap. It had begun snowing and was getting colder by the minute, and although it was only four o'clock, Bill realized he'd had enough for one day. As he sat down to enjoy a cup of café au lait, he reached into his pocket for the key. It wasn't there. He searched his pockets, but to no avail. Concerned not only about the key (which the hotel clerk had warned him not to lose because it couldn't be replaced) but also about losing face with his girlfriend, Bill was nearly frantic. Yet instead of panicking, he looked into his steaming, inviting mug of coffee, and decided that the best thing to do at the moment was to drink very slowly and relax.

Bill sat there sipping and contemplating the passing scene, refusing to give in to panic. After 45 minutes had passed, he felt the urge to get up and walk to the first metro station he'd entered that day. He remained relaxed as he trudged through the snow, which was piling up pretty fast by now. Ten paces before the metro entrance, he looked down and there, lying in the snow, was his key. It must have been there all day, and amazingly, no one had taken it. Not believing his luck, Bill picked up the key and strolled back to the café, arriving at exactly five o'clock.

His waiting girlfriend was very happy to see him, as she was loaded with packages and looking very tired. "How are you?" she asked.

"Great! Do you want some coffee?"

"No, I just want to get back to the hotel. Do you have the key?"

"Of course I do," said Bill, holding it up and smiling.

Bill still insists that what saved his butt was deciding to sit, drink, and do nothing. I agree.

My teacher Dr. Tully called downtime "incubator time." He taught me that when inspiration or guidance isn't forthcoming, if you sit still and do nothing for a minimum of two hours, guidance will show up. I've applied that rule religiously for more than 30 years, and it really works. This was how I was directed to see the dean at my university in Denver to seek entrance to the Sorbonne; how I got the inspiration to ask my husband,

Patrick, on a date instead of waiting for him to ask me; how I found the house we now live in; and how I get all my ideas for books. These are just a few of the great vibes I've gotten from giving myself a little space.

Amazing things happen when you get enough sleep, eat properly, and take it easy. Your nerve endings relax, and your spirit, or the six-sensory part of you, rejuvenates and begins to shine light on your path. This is what happens when we say that a person shines or radiates; and it's why we draw a lightbulb over a person's head to demonstrate inspiration. There's a marvelous French saying that describes this centered and solid spiritual state of awareness: *Je me sens bien dans ma peau*, or *I feel good in my skin*. We create a desirable state for all psychic systems by giving our body optimum care.

One of the most interesting things I learned in my apprenticeship with Charlie Goodman was that if your body is neglected, exhausted, or abused, it becomes energetically toxic. Your spirit actually leaves via what's known as the "silver cord" (a shimmering cord of light extending from your solar plexus to your auric field), and your psychic engines shut down.

Not willing to be trapped in such limbo, your spirit hovers outside your physical body—and when this happens, you appear dull, flat, and ashen, and it looks like nobody's home. On a soul level, nobody *is* home, so you won't feel much inspiration. That explains the saying "the lights are on, but no one's home" when describing a person who's not taking care of himself and being stupid about it. That expression is intuitively correct.

Even if you think that you're getting away with something when you abuse your body by using drugs, drinking too much, or even smoking cigarettes, you're just kidding yourself. Your body can't live in corrupted energy. It will tell you the truth by becoming weak and losing your aura (the energy field that surrounds your body and protects you). This allows negative energies and entities to move in, and, believe me, when this happens there's nothing "high" about that vibration. I see this all the time when I read for clients: They may think that they're sitting alone in the chair during a reading, but often they really aren't.

As I look psychically at these individuals, I see a crowd of little psychic critters camping out in their auras. These stowaways are lower-vibration energies composed of the generic residue of mass thinking, including general malaise, cynicism, judgment, and paranoia, and they have the ability to drive us into a funk.

If you abuse or neglect your body often enough, it's as if you're living in an abandoned home—"energy squatters" will move in and drag you down. The way to get rid of these unhappy campers is to become responsible for your body by giving it the remedy of rest, proper food, and downtime. In addition, a good Epsom-salt bath works wonders for psychic housekeeping, for the salt clears your aura of interlopers and cleanses you of what's not yours.

Psychic neglect and debris is epidemic in our fast-paced corporate world of more, more, more—which translates into less, less, less of what we need. People are unaware of how delicate the spirit is and how it needs a safe and grounded home in the body. They don't realize the price they pay by locking out their spirits. I can see it, and it looks like a picture with the color washed out. Since your body is the temple for your spirit, it's important to use common sense in caring for it; otherwise, you'll become lost, confused, and depressed.

Your vibes are always broadcasting; hearing or sensing them, however, in the whirlwind of daily life is only possible when you're in good form and spirits and when you run your life on a foundation of common sense. Despite what ego-based rules will tell you, even being six-sensory doesn't eliminate your basic responsibilities. The better you care for yourself, the more aware you'll be . . . and this is the base on which a six-sensory life rests.

Six-Sensory Practice

Start checking in with your body. In the care department, how are you measuring up? Are you getting enough sleep? If you've been meaning to go to bed earlier, now is the time to start. Even if it's only 15 extra minutes, it will make a difference. If you've been careless about what you eat, make a food plan. Decide in advance what you want and shop for it. Stock up on things that are good for you, such as veggies and grains, and prepare them so that they're ready to grab and go. Simmer soup in a big pot and eat it all week. Plan at least one balanced, fresh meal a day, and make it. Give up that fourth cup of coffee and the Milk Duds, and have some blueberries instead (which I just read are one of nature's perfect foods).

If you aren't sleeping well, turn off the nightly news, get a better pillow, and take a warm, relaxing bath before you retire. Don't schedule every single moment; instead, leave some holes here and there to just hang loose. Take vitamins, but don't overdo it: One-a-day tablets will do, so don't take six. Get your appointment book out and schedule do-nothing-but-relax periods during the week, and then *keep* those appointments. Be sensitive to what your body needs and make peace with it—for example, go to the bathroom when you need to instead of postponing it until you finish a project. And drink at least six glasses of water a day. My teacher Charlie told me that the psychic sense is like a battery that needs water to charge itself.

Don't be irresponsible or negligent about your basic needs, but don't be too dramatic about it, either—a few simple efforts will go a long way toward living a higher life. It's all in the attitude: A five- sensory attitude says to hurry up and do more, while a six-sensory attitude says that all this responsible care is necessary for your temple.

SIX-SENSORY WISDOM:

Take good care of yourself.

(P.S. If you have addictions, not only do they ruin your sixth sense, they ruin everything else as well. Keep in mind that as you reach for higher ground, it's necessary to leave the swamp. Before you can go one step further, you must be honest and admit you need help. Then get it. It's time.)

SECRET #3

You must be grounded to listen to and start trusting your vibes. This means that you need to be connected to your body and to the support of the earth. When you aren't grounded, you can't draw enough energy to activate your higher awareness—as if you're a lamp that isn't plugged in to an outlet. As a result, your sixth sense shuts down; and you lapse into anxiety, worry, and restlessness.

You know you're ungrounded when you fall out of touch with reality and experience any or all of the following: You exaggerate your problems, fret over imagined things, or act like a drama queen; you feel insecure, out of sorts, restless, or ineffective; you drop the ball, trip over your feet, go in circles, or repeat yourself for no reason; you can't focus or concentrate; or you spend a lot of energy accomplishing very little.

When you're not grounded, your energy gets blocked at your feet and can't rise to your heart (the seat of your sixth sense), causing you to spin your wheels. You can also be ungrounded in reverse when you get stuck in your head and can't feel your heart center. This completely cuts you off from your intuition, like a hamster caught in an endless cycle on its exercise wheel. The result is that you're denied access to the support of the earth *and* the higher awareness of your spirit, leaving you in a mental and emotional knot.

Being grounded is basic to tuning in to your vibes. Because our bodies follow spiritual law, they require, like all things in nature, a connection to Mother Earth to function. Grounding makes that connection. Your ego has no connection to any support other than its own fear—it's neither connected to the Divine Father nor the Divine Mother, so it will try to convince you that you don't need either of them to exist. This is insane. Like a cut flower in a vase, we'd perish if we were disconnected from our source.

I must admit that this has been one of the hardest lessons for me to learn. I get caught up in things and forget to get out of my head as much as anyone else does, even though I know it's a mistake to do so. When I'm ungrounded, I can't hear my vibes, so I become too emotional, defensive, and crabby. And always, to my frustration, becoming ungrounded sneaks up on me just as it will with you.

You know the signs. *Stage one:* You get a little anxious. *Stage two:* You start getting crabby. *Stage three:* You begin to waste energy letting everyone know how you feel. *Stage four:* You lose your cool altogether and become unglued, unfocused, or just plain unhappy. The key is to pay attention to these little shifts before you unravel.

Fortunately, the way to get regrounded and plug back in to Universal support is simple: Just get back into your body by doing something physical. Every time you feel out of touch with the world, or you intuitively shut down because of the burden of trying to figure things out, go outside and take a brisk walk for 15 to 20 minutes. Refocusing your attention on physical activity takes you back into Divine flow and begins to provide your body with the life force it needs to raise your vibration and activate your psychic channel.

If your body were a computer, being ungrounded would be like freezing up, whereas doing something physical is the energetic equivalent of rebooting the system. Going outside and walking, or doing some other physical activity, interrupts this energy glitch, resets your energy system, and gets everything moving in the right direction again. It will calm you down and ground you.

Physical activity also expels any accumulated negative or overloaded energy in your aura. In the same way that a lightning storm affects the atmosphere, exercise clears away psychic pollution, refreshes your system, and unclutters your point of view. For example, my teacher Charlie would habitually go for a brisk 30-minute walk before he met his clients for a reading. This cleared his energy field of any negative psychic debris he may have accumulated during the day, and his awareness would then be free from all distractions. After his walk, he could better tune in to his psychic sense and guide his clients. (I've followed his example by walking to the gym.)

Grounding gets your energy flowing in one direction and keeps you from getting in your own way. It quiets your internal chatter so that you can hear the subtle voices of your angels and guides, who can then offer solutions to challenges. Otherwise, they'd be unable to get past your thoughts.

Shifting your energy from a mental to a physical focus can jump-start your creativity as well, especially if you're stuck. I have a client who wanted to be a screenwriter, yet she couldn't write a single sentence worth reading when she went to her screenwriting class or tried to create at home. But once she took up running, entire scripts started streaming into her brain from the heavens. She'd run through the park, and then run home as fast as she could to capture her inspired stories on paper.

I have another client who dreamed of being a songwriter, and he told me that every time he hit a creative block, he blasted through it by going to the local YMCA and shooting baskets. After two or three weeks of basketball, new songs came flying out of him like skyrockets on the Fourth of July.

Getting in sync with the flow of the Universe doesn't mean that you have to join a gym and get in shape, although it certainly helps. It simply means that if you want to access your vibes, you need to give your mind a break and take your body outside.

Some of my greatest psychic guidance has come to me when I've been out walking or riding my bike. In fact, my book *The Wise Child* was channeled after I took an early-morning bike ride along the Chicago lakefront one summer several years ago. I didn't have a clue about what to write before I went for my ride— but the minute I came back, my pen took off across the paper as the ideas poured in.

I often think that the reason two people may not get along or are unable to understand one another is because at least one of them is simply ungrounded. The wisest, most effective way to solve the problem may be to go for a walk so that both of you can move your energy into your hearts and reestablish a rapport.

I discovered this secret by accident during a particularly stressful and ungrounded period in my life, and I'm glad I did. My husband, Patrick, and I were in the middle of a major house renovation that became far more complicated than we were prepared for. Our stress erupted into daily arguments that exacerbated our problems and further alienated us. Because we were renting a small apartment at the time and didn't want our landlord to overhear our quarrels, we took them outside. We continually engaged in combat in one spot, but soon felt compelled to walk so that we wouldn't make a scene in front of the neighbors. As we did, an amazing thing happened: We stopped arguing. The more Patrick and I walked, the calmer, more centered, and open to each other we became. We began to intuitively feel that everything would settle down and work out fine. Soon our walks transformed from squabbles into creative brainstorming sessions. By getting grounded, we corralled all that energy and used it to access our vibes instead of picking on each other. The challenges remained, but our relationship actually ended up becoming stronger.

Not only is being physically grounded a solid requirement for tuning in to your vibes, it's also an instant antidote for obsession or worry. Whenever you find yourself overly concerned or unable to stop thinking about something, immediately go outside and walk; or better yet, run around the block to disrupt the toxic trance you're in. I've never known anyone to find answers from thinking things to death, but I *have* known people who gained peaceful insights and grand solutions while strolling through the park.

Six-Sensory Practice

This week, exercise or do something physical every day for at least 15 minutes. Start with a short walk around the block and then build up to more rigorous efforts. During this time, simply enjoy yourself and allow your mind to relax. Notice how negative energy starts to drain out of your body, leaving you more relaxed. You can amplify this effect by releasing all anxiety and worry and restoring your health and vitality with every deep breath you take.

Observe how physical activity affects your intuition and awareness. Everything will appear more clear after you go for a walk than it will while you're sitting in your office all day. Doing something physical restores psychic clarity in ways you aren't even conscious of, so remember to expel accumulated energy through physical effort. In this way, your mind will stay clear, your aura will be cleansed, and your attention will remain sharp.

SIX-SENSORY WISDOM:

Go outside.

SECRET #4

LISTEN TO YOUR BODY

Perhaps the most immediate way to tune in to your vibes is by listening to and understanding the psychic feedback of your physical body. Your vibes try to reach you first through your physical body because the mind follows ego law and, therefore, has the capacity to filter out and distort information, or convince you that it's okay to do what's actually harmful. The body is actually part of your Divine self, so it follows spiritual law. It honestly and accurately reflects how energy impacts you on a vibrational level through physical signals—such as aches, pains, flutters, ripples, tightness, fatigue, or even sickness. The particular signal depends on what it's trying to tell you.

Not only is the body an honest six-sensory channel, it's also fairly straightforward. In other words, if you're on the right track doing what serves your soul, then you're going to feel good, relaxed, and peaceful. Your heart will beat steadily, your energy will remain high, and you'll be relatively free from aches, pains, anxiety, or stress. If, on the other hand, you're making poor choices that compromise your spirit, or if you find yourself in circumstances that threaten or disrupt your psychic well-being, your body will communicate this as well.

If you heed these signals and make the necessary adjustments to restore safety and balance, your body will relax and return to a quiet, more stress-free state.

However, if you ignore these signals and allow your ego to take over and continue to do what disturbs your peace, especially over a long period of time, your physical body will turn up the volume and hammer away at your attention, resulting in greater tension, physical pain, insomnia, or any number of physical disturbances. And if you ignore your body's signals completely, there's a good chance that you could become severely ill or depressed.

Fortunately, your body's signals are simple to read. It's mostly a matter of deduction: For example, problems with your legs usually reflect where you're going in life, or whether you can stand on your own two feet. Problems with your sexual organs and lower abdomen often reflect blocked creativity or an absence of pleasure and sexuality. Gastrointestinal difficulties reflect a feeling of being overwhelmed, as if you're unable to digest life or "stomach" certain conditions. Heart concerns are often associated with your ability to give and receive love easily, while the neck and throat relate to speaking your truth and listening to the world with an open mind and heart. Trouble with your eyes often points to difficulties with perception, outlook, and point of view, and brain problems reflect karmic secrets.

This, of course, is a simplified version of the language of the body—and it's certainly not intended to take the place of an adequate medical diagnosis—but it shows how you can make the connection between your psychic state and your physical experiences. (You can find out more about how various parts of the body correspond to psychic and emotional balance in my book *True Balance*. In the meantime, just observe—your body will directly tell you what's wrong.)

Even though there are some generic similarities in everyone's psychic-feedback system, each of us has our own unique set of signals. When I'm facing something potentially dangerous or negative, my body warns me by giving me a sharp pain in my temples. The minute I get this signal, I know that I'm into something I should avoid, so I do. My husband doesn't get his signals in the same way. When he feels that something isn't right for him, he becomes intensely restless—his vibes urge him to leave.

When I was young and my mother felt that something wasn't right for her (or was "off," as she called it), she got a buzz in her ears. I remember dozens of times being in the middle of a sentence, and she'd shush me because her ears started ringing with a warning that she needed to pay attention to.

My psychic friend LuAnn becomes weak when she encounters anything psychically compromising or dangerous to her. Her body simply stops moving forward. "When this happens," she says, "no matter what my brain wants to do, my legs simply won't move." On the other hand, my friend Joan receives *positive* intuitive signals by getting goose bumps, which tell her that she's on the right track and all systems are go.

In reading for clients, I've observed that their fatigue is often a very strong signal that a situation is seriously unhealthy and should be abandoned immediately. For example, after taking a job in a research laboratory, one of my clients became extremely exhausted—she'd sleep 12 hours a day and still feel tired. Not only did she hate her job because it was boring, but there were dangerous toxic substances in the lab. However, her ego ignored everything, saying that she needed the money more than she needed to be safe. But her body didn't miss the warning signs— eventually, this woman overslept, was late to work one day too many, and, thankfully, was fired from her unhealthy job.

Physical signals as intuitive feedback should be seen as "psychic telegrams." Again, some people get gut feelings, others feel a tightness in the chest, and still others experience a combination of vibes, such as a flutter in the throat and chills on the arms. I have a client, a successful restaurant owner, who suffers terrible digestive problems every time he gets involved with unscrupulous people, which occurs often in the restaurant business. He says, "My mind never seems to figure it out, but my gut always does. I find myself wanting to work with these characters because they're so persuasive, but my stomach doesn't buy it. It goes into a knot and won't stop until I get rid of these people."

Another client who's in sales says, "Every time I feel a lump in my chest, I know that the person I'm making a deal with isn't going to pay me. I can't explain it, and I have no other evidence at the time, but it always bears out to be true. It may take months to have that confirmed, but I know when we sign the contract—or at least my body knows."

Once you start paying attention to your body's vibes, you'll appreciate how faithfully it keeps you informed, not only about what's really going on around you, but what's going on with your body itself.

Listening to your body's signals can keep you balanced and safe. After all, your health-care practitioners and advisors are only human, so they need your help in keeping you healthy. I've spoken with several doctors over the years who admit that in some of their patients' cases, they're merely guessing at a diagnosis and can use all the help they can get in figuring out the problem. Knowing this, you can see how limiting it is to completely surrender your well-being to others, regardless of how talented they are. A far more enlightened approach to health care is a partnership with your medical experts.

Tracy, a 41-year-old client with a 6-year-old son, is another example of how strong the body's signals can be. Tracy had no luck conceiving a second child, even after numerous attempts with in vitro fertilization and fertility drugs. Frustrated and demoralized, she came in for a reading to learn what the problem was. The doctors could only guess at the trouble, but my reading showed that Tracy had no specific physical problem at all—but emotionally, she was resistant to conception. I picked up on a soul level that she'd long been concerned about world overpopulation and had made a commitment to help the problem by mothering an abandoned child. On a conscious level, she'd forgotten about this; her body, however, had not. Tracy's body had remained faithful to the commitment by not conceiving any more children of her own.

After sharing what I'd picked up, I asked her, "Does any of this make sense to you?"

Tracy was surprised, but she replied, "Yes, it does. I've always secretly felt that I should adopt a child, even before I was married. But after the birth of my son, I forgot about it. I never even discussed it with my husband. He's so set on having another baby of our own that I haven't brought it up. But I actually *do* feel guilty about continuing our efforts when in our own city, children are waiting to be parented, and I can help. It bothers me, but I've been ignoring it."

I didn't hear from Tracy for two years, at which point she sent me a note saying that she and her husband had adopted a four-year-old girl. Six months later, she notified me that they'd adopted a boy. "I don't know that having more of my own children would have been more satisfying than these kids," she wrote, "but I honestly can't imagine that it would." Her body was faithful to what her soul really wanted, even if she didn't consciously know it at the time.

I believe that no matter how confusing your body's signals may appear, they always make sense if you just listen and learn its language. Listening to your body's vibes for guidance and feedback may seem odd at first, but keep in mind that your body is a direct conduit for your Higher Self, and it won't mislead you. Every signal it sends has direct meaning and important information for both your physical well-being and your spiritual balance and safety. It doesn't take a mystic to read and understand your body's messages—after all, it's *your* body. The more you pay attention to it and want to understand what it's trying to convey, the easier it becomes.

You should always interpret your body signals carefully. If you have a bellyache every time you go to work, perhaps it's telling you not to go. If you can't sleep at night, perhaps your body can't get your attention during the day. If you get tired every time you go out on a date with someone, perhaps that person is draining you. It doesn't take a detective to figure it out—just a little attention.

Remember, unless you begin to trust your vibes as they move through your body, you'll never experience a higher, more peaceful way of life. But if you do, you can access your inner healer immediately. It's your choice.

Six-Sensory Practice

This week, listen to your body. Every morning as you wake up, run a mental scanner over yourself from head to toe and see if you're getting any signals. Do you have any psychic telegrams in the form of aches, pains, illness, or tension? If so, what are they telling you? Acknowledge what you're feeling and tell your body, "I'm listening."

While taking your shower, talk to your body and check in with what's going on. Ask if it wants you to know anything important that you haven't noticed before, and let it know that you're now paying attention. If you've been cursing your body, or rejecting or criticizing it, stop, because you're really hurting yourself. Your body is your ally, so quit attacking it, or it won't be able to help you. Don't shoot the messenger—after all, your body can only work with what you give it, and it's just trying to protect you either from yourself or something in your world.

If you have a particular physical challenge, ask your body what you can do to ease the problem. Resist the temptation to dismiss this as a waste of time. Dr. David Edelberg, one of Chicago's most respected physicians, once told me that after 35 years of medical practice, he's observed that the best way to stay healthy is to talk to your body first: "It's the best diagnostician I know."

Don't feel as if you're imagining things when your body talks to you—even if you are, what you're imagining will have meaning. Pay close attention, and voice these messages out loud so that you can actually hear what your body is saying. Sometimes the more you speak out loud, the more your body's messages will come through.

Heed any signals your body sends you throughout the day. Be alert for any tension, tightness, rumbles, tickles, flickers, uneasiness, pain, loss or surge of energy, or fits of restlessness—and see if they correlate to the situation you're in. Does the tightness in your chest correspond to entering your workplace? Does the burst of energy you feel have anything to do with the great new friend you just met or the class you enrolled in? Notice how your body communicates the red and green lights of psychic feedback, and don't censor or dismiss a thing.

Opening a dialogue with your body is the beginning of creating better physical and psychic health. If you listen, your sixth sense will guide you.

SIX-SENSORY WISDOM:

Your body knows.

PART II

Mind Over Matter

SECRET #5

I f you want to learn to trust your vibes, you must maintain a peaceful and relatively calm attitude. When you're tense, nervous, or anxious, your energy gets tangled up and blocked and can't enter your heart center, where your Higher Self and your vibes communicate.

Remaining calm no matter what's going on around you is an incredible challenge, but it will liberate your psychic sense and will probably add a few years to your life as well—after all, getting worked up about things only makes them worse. Life is always full of drama and challenges, but you don't have to overreact to any of it if you choose not to. You have the option of moving from being an emotion-laden reactor to a curious, aware observer.

Martial-arts students are taught that their best defense is to maintain a calm state of mind so they can sense trouble before it occurs and step out of harm's way instead of running head-on into it. If you pay close attention, you can feel trouble before it happens because disruptive psychic energy travels faster than physical energy does. But sensing this danger is only possible if you're relaxed and at ease.

Animals are good examples of this phenomenon. I read in Elaine Aron's book *The Highly Sensitive Person* that when antelopes feel a stampede, they move away 30 minutes before it arrives because they're so calm. We humans have a psychic self-defense system that's even more sophisticated, and if we don't get hysterical every time something challenging happens, we can access it. When we *do* become agitated and overwhelmed, it doesn't take an intuitive to see that we're creating so much commotion within ourselves that we'll misread the energy around us, let alone be open to a forewarning of trouble.

Being calm is a skill that starts with proper breathing. Dr. Tully taught me that breathing deeply and regularly is not only the key to remaining calm, but also instantly connects us to a higher vibration. When we're stressed or fearful, we tend to hold our breath, which cuts us off from our Higher Self and our intuitive vibes. Dr. Tully said that it's almost physically impossible to be uptight and breathe deeply at the same time. Try it and you'll see for yourself.

Breathing purposefully during stressful situations is intuitively intelligent, for it keeps you open to guidance rather than forcing you to succumb to a fight-or-flight stance that diminishes your awareness. Conscious breathing helps you stay in your heart and out of your head, and it raises your vibration level enough to be guided, even if your intellect doesn't have a clue what to do.

Remember *The Pink Panther* movie series? The main character, Inspector Clouseau, was a bumbling idiot, but he was also always completely calm—even as those who thought they were smarter and more sophisticated than he were continually thrown into absolute hysteria by his antics. Clouseau was grossly mistaken about the situations he was in, yet he never failed to find solutions (even if it was always by accident), while those who lost their cool, lost out. I love these movies because they brilliantly demonstrate intuition in action. In other words, you don't always have to know what you're doing—if you remain cool, calm, and connected to spirit, your intuitive vibes will direct you along the way. I've lived like this for 44 years and counting, and it works. The key is to stay relaxed and remember to breathe.

My favorite breathing technique is to inhale and then slowly exhale by saying, "Ahhhh," which immediately centers and calms me. Try it right now—you'll see that it works. Dr. Tully had me breathe like this for a few minutes every day, starting with two breaths and gradually extending it until it became second nature. It took a while, but breathing in this way is now a habit, especially when I'm under stress.

Another great breathing exercise my husband, a meditation teacher, taught me is to place one hand on my belly and the other on my chest and breathe in through my nose and out through my mouth slowly until I feel calm. If you use this stress reliever every time you're scared or unsure of action, it will signal your vibes to kick into gear and will help you attain higher ground and gain direction in minutes.

SOME PEOPLE ARE NOT ONLY HABITUALLY UPTIGHT, which keeps them from ever tuning in to their sixth sense, but they're also drama junkies who are addicted to the adrenaline that comes with the theatrical. Needless to say, a steady shot of this turmoil cuts you off from your intuitive channel and blocks it from opening. Adrenaline is a highly toxic and addictive substance if you're subjected to it in large quantities. Of course it's great when you need it for immediate action (such as when a pit bull is chasing you down the street), but it can eat you alive if you pump it into your veins every time you don't get the parking spot you want or someone cuts you off on the highway.

Besides being difficult to wean from, excessive adrenaline is to your intuition what kryptonite is to Superman: lethal. A burst of adrenaline may leave you feeling temporarily powerful, but it will end up depleting you. If you're a drama junkie, I recommend that you seriously consider the consequences: Too much adrenaline is poison—it can literally kill you if you keep it up. (It doesn't wear well, either. In case you don't know it, you appear ridiculous when you're screaming at the top of your lungs or frantically fussing over things as if contending for an Oscar for best dramatic performance. I know because I've done it, and my children have told me how idiotic it looks.)

The best antidote to an adrenaline high is a cool shower or a brisk walk. If you have the privacy, you can also detox by screaming into or beating a pillow, or hitting a punching bag.

But remember that people aren't pillows or punching bags, and blasting your tension onto them is unbelievably damaging to both of you and is also bad karma. Besides, they'll retaliate as soon as you let your guard down—you'll never know when it's coming, so this is an extremely unwise practice.

When training your mind to trust your vibes, it's important to be aware of what sends you into orbit, and if possible, eliminate it at its source. It took me years to realize that loud noises cause me to melt down instantly and slam my intuitive channel shut. It feels as if I'm being electrocuted. Unreasonable deadlines almost always cause my friend LuAnn to hyperventilate and block any intuitive inspiration, while too many commitments tie my sister Soraya into a knot and shut her vibes down. But all three of us have come up with solutions: I regulate the noise level around me, LuAnn negotiates her deadlines well in advance, and Soraya says no. What must *you* change in your life so that you're calm and peaceful? Can you? Will you?

Another spiritual suggestion for remaining calm is to refrain from trying to control everyone around you. The more controlling you are, the more you'll get lost in ego land and removed from your spirit. Of course you probably don't even notice when you're being controlling. As I've mentioned, embracing spirit is tricky, and the ego isn't about to cooperate because it knows that it's being dethroned. Therefore, sometimes it tries to fake you out and make you believe something is spiritually motivated when, in fact, it's only more of the same old ego stuff in disguise.

For example, my client Mary considered herself very spiritual, but the truth was that she rarely actually listened to her spirit—instead, she was always figuring things out in her head. She insisted that she loved her teenage children, and to show it, she got up every morning to prepare breakfast for them before school. Now this sounds very loving of her, but the kids weren't hungry and repeatedly told her so. Mary insisted that they eat anyway because of the trouble she went through to prepare food for them. The kids just fought back. Consequently, a mother's good intentions deteriorated into daily power struggles because she was being extremely controlling and got busted.

Finally, Mary stopped micromanaging and listened to her vibes for guidance. They told her to make her own breakfast and then go for a walk before the kids got up. Just thinking about doing this made her feel better, even though her brain said it was selfish. As a result, Mary's mornings became her favorite time of the day, and as for her kids, who knows? She wasn't home when they left.

One difference between spiritual and ego law is that spiritual law is very playful and creative, while ego law is fixed and routine. One way in which I incorporate a little playfulness into putting on the brakes whenever I get too controlling is to play a little game with myself. Not only do I become aware that I'm being controlling, but I've taken it a step further and have actually named my inner control freak. I call her "Snit," because that's what she goes into when life isn't going her way. My imaginary Snit is a humorless drag who even makes *me* uncomfortable. When Snit appears in my life, I know that I need to back off and take a breather. That's because she only shows up when I'm pushing myself too hard, so she starts to push back. In spite of her poor humor, Snit is actually good for me. She attempts to take care of me in a dreadful sort of way—but sadly, she doesn't succeed. When Snit's around, things only get worse.

I think we all have an inner Snit who tries to take care of us and wants something *from* us and *for* us—peace, alone time, oxygen. What is your inner Snit's name, and what does she need? Can you say yes to her? After all, your inner Snit is a vibe messenger of sorts, too, getting your attention by being noisy and unreasonable, or whatever else it takes. Give in and listen to this voice so that you can calm down.

And remember, the reason you listen to your vibes is to surrender control so that the Universe can step in and help you. God knows better than you how to take action in most situations, so relax, get out of the way, and let it happen. You'll never learn to trust your vibes if you're in a snit, at least not as a way of life. We all have moments when we need to blow our fuse and release passion, but to bulldoze through life ready to mow down anything in your path at the slightest provocation will not only cut you off from your heart and intuition, it could actually give you a heart *attack*. In other words, running the world when no one asked you to is not only fatal to trusting your vibes, it can be fatal on other levels, too.

Six-Sensory Practice

This week, lighten up and go with the flow. Begin each day with deep breathing—inhale and then exhale to the sound of "Ahhhh," and repeat this for a minute or two. And when you're in stressful situations, remember to place your hands over your belly and chest and breathe in through your nose and out through your mouth. If possible, get a relaxing massage; if you can't, then take a bubble bath every night and stay in the tub long enough to unwind.

Imagine that you're an easygoing person, even if this is new for you. You can be a beginner and still be calm. To fuel your new and more enlightened self-image, watch movies with characters who stay tranquil under pressure, such as *The Pink Panther* or *Cool Hand Luke*—take notes, and imitate them. If you get into any ridiculous arguments, try to remember to back off and *breathe*. And if you're really brave, say "You win," and drop it. (I know this one is challenging, but try it.) It's worth it. But if you can't quite pull it off, don't worry about it. We're striving for progress, not mastery.

Name your inner control freak and figure out what brings her around: Fear? Insecurity (usually the biggest culprit)? Restlessness? Get to know what your inner Snit wants so that you can give it to her and cut her off at the pass. Take notes—you'll need them, because you'll forget what she said. Practice sensing tension in the air like an antelope, and move away from it instead of heading straight for it. Remember to breathe as you do this. Also, go to bed early, secure in the knowledge that God is in control, not you. Sleep tight.

Tension-Buster Bonus

Practice tightly tensing your muscles: Hold them for ten seconds, then release them to restore calm. Start with your neck and shoulders and the muscles in your face: Tense, hold, release. Move to the muscles in your stomach, chest, and back: Tense, hold, release. Go to the muscles in your buttocks: Tense, hold, release. Finally, tense the muscles in your legs and feet: Tense, hold, release. When you finish tensing all the muscles in your body, shake them out, as if you were a bowl of Jell-O, and let out a few belly sounds, such as "Aaaah," or "Ooohhh." Repeat until you feel all the tension in your body drain away. Notice how much more aware you are when you're not tense. Enjoy.

SIX-SENSORY WISDOM:

Take it easy.

SECRET #6

QUIET, PLEASE

In order to trust your vibes, you have to first be able to sense them—and to do this, you must quiet your mind. You see, your sixth sense is very subtle and noninvasive, and even though it's always present, it's very discreet and dignified and will never interrupt or interfere with your internal chatter. It's not that your Higher Self is reticent or shy; it's just that until you mentally shut up, you can't hear what it has to say. Just as if you try to listen to two people talk at the same time, you can't hear your vibes if your ego is clamoring over your spirit for all the attention. So it's not only spiritually smart to quiet down, it makes practical sense as well. The key is to be creative as you look for silence in the world.

For example, Kim, a client of mine who's a sales representative for a pharmaceutical company, had to drive 40 miles to work twice a week. She liked to commute with the radio turned off so that she could "have a little peace," as she put it. During these drives, she often got intuitive flashes that popped into her brain like telegrams. Once, she even got a flash that compelled her to request a transfer to San Francisco.

Kim had wanted to make this move for years, but she was continually told it wasn't possible because that office had no openings. Even though her message flew in the face of what she'd been told at work, she listened anyway. "Okay, I will," she said aloud to her inner voice.

Kim put in her transfer that afternoon, and later that day, the San Francisco office unexpectedly opened up to transfers for the first time. The company only transferred two people, and hers was the first request. As Kim later told me, "Had it not been for my quiet drive, I'm positive that I would have missed my opportunity. It was the quiet that allowed me to hear my Higher Self loud enough to follow it."

My brother-in-law Gene, who's a master carpenter and craftsman, recently developed a love and talent for creating sculptures. He's fashioned some beautiful granite-and-steel works of art, one of which sits in our garden. When I asked him how he gets his inspiration, he said that in the night, when everyone is asleep and the house is so quiet you can hear a pin drop, he gets visions. "All of a sudden, I see these sculptures in my mind's eye in three dimensions," he explained. "I walk around them and study them very carefully. I can almost touch them, they feel so clear. Then I can re-create what I see. But the visions only appear when it's completely silent."

Over the years I've received many unexpected intuitive messages in quiet moments. A favorite memory is when Eric, a close friend from France, called sometime ago to tell me that his father, Serge, had suddenly died. Serge was someone I had loved dearly; in fact, it was his family that had taken me in when I was a student at the Sorbonne years ago. Eric was devastated by his father's death—and since he was on his way to Chicago for business later that week, I invited him to dinner.

Before Eric arrived, I took a 20-minute rest in one of our living room chairs. Not quite awake, but not quite asleep (I was in what I call my "alpha state"), I clearly heard twice in my mind, "Cherry clafouti." I knew that cherry clafouti was a French dessert, but I didn't know anything else about it. I wondered why I was hearing this, since I'd never had the dessert or even thought about it. Nevertheless, it sounded interesting. When I roused myself, Patrick, my husband and our resident chef, asked what I thought he should make for dessert. Without thinking, I said, "Cherry clafouti."

"What's that?" he asked.

"I don't know, but doesn't it sound good? I think I dreamed about it."

Inspired by the challenge, Patrick found a recipe and made the dessert. During dinner, Eric was quite emotional, especially because he hadn't been able to say good-bye to his dad and tell him how much he loved him. After dinner, I wanted to comfort my friend, so I said, "Well, Eric, I know this won't necessarily cheer you up, but we have a special dessert for you this evening—cherry clafouti. How does that sound?"

Eric nearly jumped out of his chair. "Mon dieu!" he cried, stunned. "Cherry clafouti was my father's favorite dessert. He adored it."

"He must be around because he ordered it himself this afternoon as I was resting," I told my heartbroken friend. It was as though Serge was telling his son that he was still near him. And somehow, that cherry clafouti offered some sort of closure that Eric hadn't felt before.

There are lots of ways to get quiet and hear your spirit, but for most people these moments are random: a few minutes tidying up, waiting for a ride, or picking someone up; or a quickly snatched catnap. But your quiet moments don't have to be stolen. You can select them, and if you want to connect to your sixth sense, you need to engage the support of your mind to choose them regularly.

My teachers taught me that the best way to ensure quiet moments is to meditate. I agree, at least in theory—I mean, I do encourage meditating in all my books. Yet, in working with so many people over the years, I've observed that most don't do it, despite all the information out there confirming how valuable this practice is. In addition to helping us tap in to our intuitive voice, meditation reduces stress, helps us feel peaceful and grounded, sharpens our senses, and increases our patience and creativity. Still, people resist, are confused about how to do it, or don't do it in the traditional way—which is to get comfortable, simply relax your mind, center your attention, and breathe peacefully and calmly for 5 to 20 minutes while emptying your brain of thought and worry.

It doesn't take talent to meditate, only patience, consistency, and reasonable expectations. If you meditate every day in the same place at the same time, then in less than two weeks your subconscious mind will get used to the idea and begin to cooperate. And then, each time you sit down to meditate, it will become easier and faster to reach the state of inner calm you seek. The key to success is not to expect anything other than giving yourself a little peace and quiet. If you think you have to drift into nirvana to be "really" meditating (which is your ego talking), you'll just get frustrated and won't succeed.

To meditate, it goes without saying that it helps to get quiet inside by creating quiet around you. This means turning off your cell phone and your regular phone; and shutting off the music, the TV, the computer, and anything else that might distract you. However, you don't necessarily have to do it in the sanctuary of your home. Several of my clients have found success in the most unlikely places. For example, Lee found her quiet moments by visiting the Episcopal church next to her office in downtown Chicago on her lunch hour, even though she wasn't Episcopalian. "Sitting in silence really centered me," she said, "and often while I sat there, I could feel my Higher Self soothing me, making life a little easier." Thom found peace in a small park near his office where he simply sat and fed the birds on his break, and Michelle paradoxically found tranquility by sitting on a bench in a busy mall, observing the world go by. "As I watched and relaxed, I stopped hearing the noise—it just faded away," she marveled.

Yet getting quiet by sitting still doesn't work for everyone. Some people are just too fired up, and meditating is too difficult for them. If you happen to fall into this category, I suggest that you not set yourself up for failure, which your ego would love. If meditation isn't for you, don't worry about it. Spiritual law is flexible and creative, and, believe me, traditional meditation has no monopoly on gaining access to your sixth sense—there are many days when even I can't do it. The solution is to work with who you are and try nontraditional, creative ways to achieve the same result. Try getting quiet by engaging your hands and doing some sort of silent task for a while. Here's an example of what I mean.

David was as restless and antsy as a person could be. He was always tapping his fingers, shaking his foot, or moving in his chair, and although meditation would clearly have been good for him, he had no luck doing it. When I did his intuitive reading, his guides suggested that he take up a hobby that would consume his attention and silence his thoughts—so David chose building model airplanes. He started small but soon found the practice so refreshing that it became his after-work passion. He spent about 45 minutes a day unwinding his brain and receiving all sorts of intuitive messages. One afternoon as he assembled the wings of an airplane, David distinctly felt his brother's energy in the room, although they hadn't spoken in years. He was so connected to this feeling that he realized how much he missed his brother and decided to call him that night. As he was about to pick up the phone, it rang—and it was his brother. He was calling to tell David that he'd just been diagnosed with prostate cancer, and even though it looked as if he was going to beat it, it made him remember what was important to him, so he wanted to reestablish contact.

I believe that the more you practice getting quiet, the quicker you'll sense your vibes. It doesn't matter what approach you use as long as you *get quiet.* Choose what suits your temperament: My mind becomes quiet when I fold laundry, organize my office, or go to the gym; Patrick paints and gardens; my mom sews; my dad putters on gadgets; my brother Stefan washes his car; one of my neighbors loves to work in the yard, while another walks his dog. All are valid ways to connect with your spirit.

The key to having quiet time is to value it. If it's important to you, you're going to find the time. The more you get quiet, the more you'll be able to hear your vibes. And the more you hear them, the more you'll trust them.

Six-Sensory Practice

This week, take 10 minutes for quiet time each day (20 if you can manage it). If you like to meditate and it isn't a struggle, then do it, for it really is the best way to tune in to your spirit and hear the voice of Divine Guidance. If traditional meditation doesn't work for you, put on your thinking cap and brainstorm other ways to get a few moments of silence every day. Examine your life carefully to discover if there are any built-in opportunities already in place. Do you drive a lot, for instance? If so, can you use this time for creating quiet? Plan your quiet time every day in advance instead of hoping to steal a few moments here and there. Notice how much easier it is to hear your sixth sense when you have more quiet moments, and reflect on how much peace this brings to your life.

SIX-SENSORY WISDOM:

Listen.

SECRET #7

OBSERVE, DON'T ABSORB

I t's not enough that your sixth sense works; you want it to work *well*. Why? Because unless you're selective, you may unwittingly tune in to what you don't want. Psychic airwaves are like radio frequencies, broadcasting many levels of information at the same time. Think of the signals from your Higher Self as the psychic equivalent of a classical station—that is, a useful channel for high, spiritual healing; while what I call "psychic riffraff"—or the generic relay of other people's feelings, moods, fears, thoughts, anxieties, and even nightmares— is the psychic equivalent of talk radio.

If your intuitive channel is open but your tuner isn't dialed to your Higher Self, you may accidentally pick up on that negative energy without even knowing it. You may unconsciously tune in to another's anxiety, depression, or fear, and absorb it as your own, which will cause you to become depressed and perhaps paranoid. Or you may absorb someone else's anxiety, anger, and even illness, and suddenly feel irritated and drained for no reason. As one client wondered in despair, "Sonia, I think I'm channeling everyone on the subway! By the time I arrive at work, I feel as if I'm carrying all their aches and pains and worries in my body." She was—believe it or not. Psychic absorption is real, common, and extremely infectious.

Have you ever been around a very anxious, agitated person? How long does it take before you find yourself infected with the same bug? Even if you were feeling perfectly well before contact, you may suddenly become overwhelmed by the same funk. To avoid this "psychic contamination," stay focused and committed to your own priorities and goals. The more defined your aims are, the stronger your psychic boundaries will become, and the more insulated you'll be from any unwanted influences.

Just as you have no trouble keeping your distance from someone who has the flu, so too should you keep your psychic distance from someone who's having an "ick attack" (my term for an agitated person or unpleasant vibration), or from someone who doesn't feel energetically healthy. Even though this is simply common sense, I have to remember to do it myself. When I'm around a stressed person, I can absorb their anxiety in about three minutes. It's like catching a psychic virus. This often happens when I go to my local post office. It's as if there's some sort of psychic infection in there, and the minute I walk in, my entire body seizes up in self-defense. The building itself is old, dark, dreary, and depressing, and the people who work there are clearly affected by its terrible vibrations, for they're careless, rude, and disinterested. And this infection spreads throughout the crowd waiting in line. Unless I shield myself from this energy, by the time I leave I'm in such a bad mood I can chew nails.

I like going to this post office, however, because it gives me a chance to practice what I preach. I decide in advance to observe and not absorb, and to have compassion for those infected with the "funk vibe" while I'm there. Some days are better than others, and I've learned not to go at all if I'm not feeling well because it's a recipe for disaster. But when I'm in good spirits, I can remain detached.

You too can practice detachment so you can stay psychically centered in the midst of a lot of energy, such as when you're at the airport, eating in a busy restaurant, sitting in a crowded movie theater, visiting a hospital, attending a sporting event, utilizing public transportation, working at your office, and the hardest one of all—sharing holidays with your family. These are all occasions when you might be inclined to absorb what isn't yours and lose your balance. As you practice, it helps to keep this secret in mind as a mantra—"Observe, don't absorb"—until it becomes habit.

When I was a student training with my teacher Charlie, he had me look at photographs and drawings of intensely emotional scenes, from newborn babies to people running from burning buildings and everything in between, while remaining detached. My assignment was to study these images without becoming emotionally influenced. Until I could do this, there was the risk that the energy they emitted would override my vibes and confuse me.

Because some of the pictures were extremely intense, it took months for me to study the scenes and remain neutral, instead of throwing my emotions into the mix. Day after day, Charlie would toss me a photo of something horrible or bizarre, and I'd recoil, squealing, "Oh my God! How awful!" He'd agree and laugh, but say that it wasn't necessary to get my emotions involved.

I worried that in being unemotional, it would mean that I didn't care, but strangely enough, the opposite happened: The less emotional or judgmental I was, the more accurately I could tune in to my intuition for guidance and at the same time feel compassion and love for my fellow human beings. Yet when I was more reactionary, my vibes didn't work, so I felt neither.

When I think of the challenges in my life and my struggle to remain detached, I often think of rescue workers and how selfless they need to be in order to dive into life's horrors and help the victims without getting emotionally overwhelmed. I'm humbled by those incredible and masterful souls—what would we do without them? This was what Charlie was teaching me, and the rescue workers of the world are my role models. God bless them.

My training in detachment proved to be a tremendous help in my intuitive practice. Now, no matter how emotional or distraught a client is, or how intense a situation becomes, I remain detached so that I can find answers instead of getting caught up in the drama and confusion of the moment.

I recently met with a woman named Darlene who was very angry at her abusive boyfriend. Through buckets of tears, Darlene gave me her side of the story, which included his threatening her, taking her money, snooping into her personal effects, and constantly accusing her of things. He certainly sounded like a maniac who should have been locked up.

On an emotional level, I wanted to have this guy arrested. Yet, remaining neutral, I used my sixth sense to look deeper into the problem. This time I discovered another scenario, one that didn't correspond at all with Darlene's version. I saw that even though her boyfriend was no prize, he did love her and had accurately told her that she had a serious addiction to pain medication, alcohol, and spending, and unless she sobered up, he would leave her. Her habits were out of control, and he was trying to keep her from ruining his life, too.

Granted, he was completely enmeshed in her life and unbearably controlling, but he didn't deserve to go to jail like she wanted me to believe. I suggested that she detox and he get some counseling—and she proceeded to get as angry with me as she was with him. She was in serious psychic distress, but not for the reasons she'd stated. Yet had I sympathized with her emotional state, I may have missed the real problem and the opportunity to help her.

Learning to detach is a difficult skill for those of us who are naturally six-sensory. In picking up vibes, we tend to pick up *everything,* and it takes serious focus to avoid doing so. Because some people accuse me of being insensitive when I advise them, it's important to understand that staying detached in the face of intense emotional energy doesn't mean that I don't care. It just lets me open my heart more so I can psychically see how best to respond.

It's a myth that caring requires commiserating. Caring means allowing someone space to sort things out without throwing your emotions into the already-overloaded mix. It's also important to listen to your vibes and not overtax your system. If you're bothered by the clerk at the dry cleaner, the rude guy at the grocery store, or the other passengers on the train, then don't frequent those places. Whenever you can, remove yourself from problems, and practice detachment when you can't. (And in either case, try to maintain your sense of humor!)

My favorite technique for detaching is to imagine that the world around me is a wonderful movie to learn from and enjoy, but I'm not the star of it. Just as I'd never be so lost in a film that I'd jump out of my seat and run toward the screen, so too do I restrain myself from feeling the urge to absorb the energies around me and call them my own. Using this technique, I can observe the events around me with creative detachment. The same thing may happen to you. If you get embroiled in the negativity around you, just remind yourself that it's only your movie—it's not *you*. It will pass.

Protect Yourself

One of the best ways to remain grounded in your own energy whenever exposed to an intense emotional outburst is to cover your solar plexus (the area right around your belly button) with your arms folded, which is something we tend to do anyway. Notice how natural it is to cross your arms over your stomach whenever you feel defensive. I was reminded of this instinctive protective maneuver in an airport recently while I waited for my flight. I saw a child of about two being reprimanded by his overwrought mother, and as she scolded him, he looked directly at her with his arms folded defiantly across his chest, unfazed by her outburst. He was so effective in blocking her tirade that I had to laugh.

As that child demonstrated, folding your arms across your chest or belly button blocks negative energy from entering your body and protects you from its debilitating effects. Breathing as you do this also keeps foreign energy from invading your aura, and the more slowly you breathe, the more grounded and protected you are.

Another way to prevent unwanted energy from influencing you is to actually turn away from it. If someone is upset, simply turn your body so that you're not face-to-face with them, and breathe. Energy enters into your body through your belly button, so when you turn away, you'll deflect this energy. Reminding yourself that it's not your movie—along with breathing, turning away, and folding your arms across your stomach—usually does the trick, no matter how bad the situation is.

If you aren't consciously aware of absorbing someone else's energy, pay closer attention to your vibes and then ask yourself if they are, in fact, *your* vibes. The depression or anxiety you're feeling may not really be your own; it may be the result of absorbing too much of what's around you. For example, I once had a client who worked nights at a prison and, as a consequence, was severely depressed. When she quit and began working in a church, her depression immediately lifted. The energy at the prison was simply too much to endure—in her quest to serve society, she was much better off doing so in the church.

Another way to keep others' energy from invading you is to stop whatever you're doing and name everything you see around you, out loud if possible, for at least five minutes. Right now, you might look around you and say, "I see a black desk lamp, a beige telephone, three magazines, a white vase with a red carnation in it, three pencils, a brown wastebasket, my boss smiling at a client," and so on. Continue doing this for three or four minutes, or until you're completely relaxed, calm, and neutral. This exercise trains you to get out of your head and into what's actually in front of you, instead of being emotionally hijacked into your own or someone else's drama.

The benefits of detachment in the face of intense emotional activity can't be overstated. It doesn't cut you off from your heart center; it opens you more. In fact, when you refrain from absorbing the energy around you, you'll remain clear and grounded, you'll be able to easily access your creative and intuitive channel, and you'll be able to choose to use the messages you receive from your Higher Self.

Six-Sensory Practice

This week, find the time to watch several movies in order to practice observing without getting caught up in the drama. Choose several themes, from love story to action to suspense and even comedy. If you find yourself losing ground, fold your arms over your belly and breathe; or get up and move around if you're becoming too swept up in the vibration the movie is creating.

See how much you resonate with the actors' energy. Be patient and keep your mind focused on remaining neutral, while at the same time appreciating what's going on. Study your reaction to the various themes and think about why you may remain neutral in some areas while losing yourself in others. Ask yourself if you react the same way to real-life dramas as you do to the movies.

Practice being objective, and observe how much more intuitive you are when you're neutral. Finally, see if you can predict the outcome of the films from this more objective state of mind. It's fun, and a great way to strengthen your intuitive channel.

SIX-SENSORY WISDOM:

Remember: "It's not my movie."

PART III

Good Vibrations

SECRET #8

THE SWEET SOUND OF SUCCESS

Words are powerful energies that, once released, can create the conditions and circumstances of your life like magic wands. Every word you utter has a particular vibration, tone, and intention that attracts its equivalent on the earthly plane.

Words contain the potential for you to enhance your life: They can be used to sow seeds of destruction or germinate gorgeous, flowering experiences. What you say to yourself and others lays the foundation of your life, and if you want to live in a higher way, one that is guided by your spirit and goes with the flow, you must set the tone by using loving and creative words spoken in a peaceful and harmonious voice.

My spiritual teachers taught me the importance of words early in my apprenticeship. I learned that we are all Divine Beings, co-creators with the Universe, and the foundation of our life is built through our words. Nothing we say is ever lost or impotent—in fact, each word is powerful beyond belief and commands the Universe to obey. As far as the Universe is concerned, what we say is law because it doesn't differentiate between truth and lies. It takes everything we say as truth and strives to make it so.

Have you ever called in sick to work because you wanted a free day, only to find yourself actually feeling under the weather before the day ended? Or have you ever made up an excuse to avoid dealing with someone, only to have it blow up in your face? I certainly have. Once when I was a teenager I cancelled a date with a guy I didn't really want to go out with by telling him that I had to babysit. Out of guilt, I told him several times that I was really sorry and I wished that I could see him. As soon as I got off the phone, I joined my girlfriends ice skating downtown. I was on my third twirl around the rink when I found myself nose-to-nose with the very guy I'd just broken my date with. "Babysitting, huh?" he snarled at me before skating off. Feeling stupid and embarrassed, I couldn't help but think that I had it coming, because I *did* say that I really wished I could see him . . . I guess the Universe just thought that I meant it.

Be mindful not only of what you say, but of *how* you say it, too, because the Universe is built on sound and intention. The more peaceful your words are, the higher your intention is, and the better your creation can be. Too many harsh, dissonant, and angry words—even if you believe that they represent your true feelings—have a destructive impact on yourself and others.

This was a hard lesson for my client Jennie to learn. She'd gone to a therapist who encouraged her to find her voice and speak her truth. With this therapist's coaching, Jennie began telling everybody exactly what she felt in exactly the way she felt it. She lashed out at her husband, telling him that she didn't like his hair, his breath, his taste in clothes, or his manners. She then told her in-laws to mind their own business. Gaining momentum, and feeling proud of her newly emancipated honesty, she told her boss that his ideas were old-fashioned and that she wanted more money. Believing that she was becoming a more empowered and liberated woman, Jennie was stunned when she lost her job, her husband moved out, and her son went to live with her in-laws. She'd been honest, so she couldn't understand why her life hadn't improved. After all, her therapist had spent two years convincing Jennie that being truthful was the only way to be happy. Unfortunately, when she told everyone to take a hike, they did, leaving her behind.

The problem for the Jennies of the world is that they must be careful to discern the difference between truth and opinion.

Opinions can isolate and assault, while genuine truth, even though it may be hard to hear, never attacks anyone—instead, it fosters understanding and mutual respect. In other words, being truthful means speaking without hurting yourself or others. Communicating in this way is an art and a discipline, and it releases powerful vibrations that bridge hearts, build trust, attract support, and create healing. This kind of truth has a magical potency, for it allows you to actually speak your deepest desires into being.

The Universe is organized to support your true self, and the more clearly you can communicate with it, the better it can do. When we speak out of confusion, anger, blame, or victimization, those sour notes and mixed messages send the Universe scrambling in circles, wanting to help but unable to do so.

My client Madelyn constantly complained about how impossible her ex-husband, Bob, was. According to her, the man caused her endless troubles and made her life miserable. It had been ten years since their divorce, and Bob rarely called her, lived in another city, and was remarried; and as far as I could tell psychically, he hardly ever thought about her at all. Whenever they did speak, it inevitably turned into a fight because Madelyn was constantly carping at Bob, which made them both angry and defensive. Even though he'd moved on with his life, she was still stuck in the throes of drama and struggle with him.

People avoided Madelyn because she was so negative, and although she gained three minutes of pity each time she spoke to someone, she didn't gain the freedom she needed to get on with her life. She occasionally mentioned a desire to find someone new to love, but it was more like a commercial break in the Madelyn-and-her-ex-husband-saga than it was a true, focused desire. The Universe could only work with what she asked for, so it gave her more and more trouble with Bob and never introduced another man into her life.

Ask yourself how well you're communicating your desires. If words are the building blocks of your life, you can't just hurl negative and debasing words out there and expect the Taj Mahal in return.

In addition, using careless and profane speech is very debilitating over time to a six-sensory being because it creates a dissonant, negative vibration. Swearing excessively, or using vulgar
language, especially in lieu of real words, infects the soul. Although
it may seem harmless and amusing and is certainly popular,
using this kind of language actually erodes your light body and
seriously lowers your vibration. Now I'm not saying that you
need to become as pure as the driven snow. We all know that an
enthusiastic expletive is sometimes exactly the truth about how
we feel and what we mean. I'm talking about using profanity and
street slang instead of real words on a regular basis, out of habit,
or because you're too lazy, careless, or unclear to put any effort
into communicating effectively. The Universe can only work
with what you give it and the way you give it, so just remember:
Garbage out, garbage in.

All words are potent, but words spoken with love are positively irresistible. They're as powerful as magic spells and draw
the world to your front door. For example, I once had a client
who had struggled with obesity most of her life. She'd managed
to lose only a few pounds, despite careful dieting and daily exercise. She constantly referred to her body project as "losing my
fat," even though she really wasn't losing anything. Then one
day she changed her words. She began to enthusiastically say that
she was "reclaiming my beauty." This more inspiring way of
expressing her goal excited and motivated her, and she lost ten
pounds the first week after her shift in expression. She loved her
"beauty project" and moved toward it effortlessly.

Be conscientious and creative about the words you use and
the ones you listen to as well. Know that words set the stage for
coming attractions, so if you hear gossip, disengage; if someone
is being critical, be silent. Walking away from negative conversation not only keeps your vibration oscillating at a higher rate,
but it also protects others from lowering their vibrations by
removing their audience.

The best way to maintain a higher vibration is to make every
thought and word you use or listen to as loving and nurturing
as possible. There's no more direct way than this—there are no

shortcuts, bypasses, or exceptions. When someone asks you how you are, instead of mumbling, "Okay," try replying "I'm great!" or "I'm happy to be alive!" When greeting someone, say, "Isn't it a lovely day?" rather than "I'm sick of this weather." Compliment rather than complain; express gratitude for something rather than feel sorry for yourself; and appreciate someone rather than criticize—and see what happens. The energy you communicate either seeks to reach up and love, or it doesn't. And if it doesn't, you'll miss out.

Practice loving communication in very small, repetitive ways until it becomes second nature. The more mindful you are of your words and the results they bring, the quicker you'll feel your vibes waking up. You'll feel lighter, freer, and less burdened by your own expression. Your chest will expand, your shoulders will straighten, and your heart will open. Your mental chatter will quiet down, and a softer, sweeter tone will take over your inner voice, leaving you feeling more peaceful and far more creative.

Six-Sensory Practice

This week, pay attention to what you say and what you listen to. Use your words well. Don't participate in inflammatory conversation, no matter how justified, because it will throw you off track. Remember that you're intimately connected to everyone else in the world, so when you attack another person, you attack yourself. Regardless of whether or not our ego understands this, it is nevertheless true.

Speak thoughtfully with self-control, and use loving words of acceptance, forgiveness, and humor. Rehearse kind words if you have to, especially if this isn't your normal style. If expressing yourself in person is too difficult, write nurturing words and share them via e-mail, fax, love letter, memo, note, Post-It, message board, or greeting card. Don't let it end there, however. Practice saying what you mean in a way that's effective and kind, even if it doesn't feel like you. With practice, it will become second nature. Pay particular attention to avoid using popular, yet destructive expressions in a mindless way, such as: "To die for"; "I'd kill to . . ."; "How retarded"; "I'm sick of this"; "I can't afford to . . ."; and "I hate that!"

Expand your vocabulary so that you choose words that are accurate, beautiful, sensual, inspiring, thought-provoking, mysterious, and effective. Get a word-a-day calendar or a dictionary, and learn new words to better serve your intentions. Every day, add one new, interesting word to your lexicon, and use it three times that day. Then go to bed each night by saying five positive things aloud to yourself.

SIX-SENSORY WISDOM:

Watch your words.

SECRET #9

PSYCHIC PROTECTION

As a six-sensory person, it's very important that you protect yourself from negative energy *before* it gets you down. There are several steps involved in this process, including recognizing the energy, discovering who's sending it, and either dissipating it or distancing yourself from it as quickly as possible. Allow me to discuss the steps in more detail:

<u>Step #1.</u> Identify a bad vibe (my personal term for negative energy) for what it is and see how it affects you. Do you know when something's negative, and can you identify what its impact is on you? In much the same way that recognizing cold symptoms early enough allows you to treat them before they develop into something more serious, the ability to feel negativity moving in before it overtakes you can spare you a lot of psychic distress.

When I'm exposed to a bad vibe, I first notice how my breathing restricts and how my upper chest and throat tighten. I sense a heavy pressure on the back of my head or a sinking feeling in my heart. If the energy is intense, I may even start to feel panicky. These feelings signal that negativity is moving in, like pollution, smog, or even radiation, and I need to be on guard.

I've asked my clients to describe their reactions to bad vibes just to get them thinking about it. Jeanne said, "Whenever I run into bad vibes, I feel as though I'm being 'smushed.'" John told me, "The minute I'm getting bad vibes I become cranky, even rude. Maybe this is my way of fending them off." Others shared that their hearts race, their heads feel heavy, or they become immobilized.

Admitting to yourself that you're feeling these vibes at all is always the first and best line of defense—unless you do, you can't creatively solve the situation. I've never known denial to be a good way of protecting yourself against anything.

Admittedly, some bad vibes are obvious and easy to deal with, such as when your spouse yells at you or a road-rager menaces you with insulting hand gestures. However, more sinister are the vibes from psychic snipers, or those people who secretly send you their poisonous arrows of negativity, as they masquerade behind sweet facades and pleasantries. This type of bad vibe is harder to identify, especially if you're inexperienced or are unaccustomed to trusting your psychic radar.

For example, I once met a woman who persisted in trying to befriend me, but she gave me very bad vibes. She was flattering and insistent, making plans with me, showing up at my door unannounced, and frequently bringing me presents. She was even funny and at times interesting in her boorish way, and other than being boundary-challenged, she did nothing overt that smacked of danger. Yet every time we were together, I felt that I was being set up for an ambush.

Despite appearances, I knew that this "friend" wasn't good for me. (As my mother used to say, "A rotten egg is a rotten egg, even if it's decorated for Easter.") So I kept my guard up and struggled to keep my distance. Sure enough, before long she tried to steal some of my work and take credit for it as her own. Her actions were finally exposed—and getting away from her was like getting over a horrible illness.

Because psychic snipers are sneaky, you may question or even deny that there's a real problem because you have no hard evidence to back up your feeling. Don't compromise your psychic safety by falling into this ego trap. A six-sensory person needs only the evidence of feeling bad vibes as verification. If you sense that something is out of balance, however difficult it may be to verify, trust that it's real and raise your protective shield. Know that you may have to take a little heat for your suspicions, especially from five-sensory people who deny almost everything—but just ignore it.

My client Janice had extremely bad vibes around her new stepfather, Wayne, even though he seemed to be the most kind, considerate person one could ever hope to meet. One day, Janice asked her mother about Wayne's background, but because she'd married him rather impulsively, her mom only got angry and defensive and even accused Janice of being jealous. Even Janice's siblings were annoyed with her suspicions because they were all relieved that Mom had found someone and was no longer their problem.

Nevertheless, Janice was dissatisfied. She smelled a rat and said so, despite the heat she had to take for it. As I said earlier, not only will you have to reject your ego denying your intuition, but you'll have to deal with the egos of those around you as well. Anyway, eight months after the wedding, Janice was awakened by a hysterical phone call from her mother, who said that Wayne had stolen all her assets and skipped town. It turns out that this character was a con man who had been married at least eight times—and had stolen from each of his wives.

It took great control for Janice not to rub her mother's nose in the fact that she'd warned her about Wayne, but Janice took the high road. Even her siblings apologized as they struggled to help their mother put her life back together. The only vindication Janice had was that ultimately Wayne was charged with fraud by one of his wives and ended up behind bars. (Well done, Janice.)

Step #2. The second step in protecting yourself is to speak up the minute you feel any negativity. This psychically empowering step shows others that you're fully alert and paying attention, no matter what. Start by simply saying aloud, "I have bad vibes," "Something's off—this doesn't feel right," or "Suddenly I don't feel well," the instant you feel negative energy, even if it's under your breath. Sometimes just exposing bad vibes for what they are is enough to stop them, especially if they're coming from secret psychic snipers.

I once worked with a woman whose husband's secretary sent her endless negative vibes for reasons she didn't understand (or even wanted to know). Every time they spoke, the secretary was so rude, condescending, and just plain mean that it often ruined my client's entire day. She tolerated this psychic abuse for several months and then got fed up. She began to tell the secretary how her energy affected her, by saying, "Wow! Just as we started speaking, I began to feel sick. Isn't that interesting?" Or sometimes she'd remark, "Gee, as I'm talking to you, I suddenly don't feel well. I wonder why." My client was always pleasant and nonaccusatory—she simply stated what she felt and how if affected her.

The secretary was dumbfounded. At first she said, "What? Are you okay?" But then she began to wonder, "Really? I hope it's not me causing that." To which my client wholeheartedly agreed by saying, "Me, too." And just like that, the negative energy between the two women stopped.

I've spoken to many people who say that when they feel bad vibes, they don't admit it to themselves or anyone else. But that's just someone following the ego's rules, which declare that if something isn't physical, it isn't real. Spiritual law says that psychic energy is just as real as physical energy, but it's much more revealing.

My client Marianne, an environmental lawyer, told me that as she walked to her seat on a flight from Washington to Chicago in the summer of 2001, she passed four men in business class who positively gave her the creeps. *They're evil,* she thought, but before she could even think it through, she reprimanded herself for having such an impulsive judgment about people she'd never met. Not long after this encounter, men like the ones she'd seen hijacked four airplanes on September 11. "Maybe these were the same men doing a test run," she told me. "I thought of them the minute I heard what happened." I wouldn't be surprised if her instinct was correct.

Naming a bad vibe when you feel it, even if you can't finger the source, is a powerful psychic protective tool, and doing so completely aligns with spiritual law. Spiritual law doesn't ask that you deny the negative, it tells you to be honest about everything, both good and bad. You see, when you expose negative energy, it begins to back away because it feeds on darkness and secrecy and can't stand to be brought into the light. The light begins to shrink bad vibes, and in many cases, heal them altogether.

Step #3. Next, discover where the negativity is coming from. Start by checking to see if it's coming from you. If you're tired, hungry, overextended, rushed, or in any way unhappy and uncomfortable, don't be surprised if *you're* the one who's putting out bad vibes toward others (see Secret #2, page 9). Sometimes we're our own worst enemy, and simple physical neglect is all it takes to feel that the world is against us.

You may also be feeling negative vibes because you're being critical of yourself. If so, stop it! Change your focus and start to think positive things about yourself, others, and even the entire world. Negativity is infectious, but so is positive energy. Spiritual law says that you should seek higher ground with as much positive energy as possible, and you should also ask those who have good vibes to share them with you.

When you can't identify the source of bad vibes, do a little psychic sleuthing. Ask your vibes to guide you, and then pose a lot of questions, beginning with, "Are these *my* bad vibes, or are they coming from someone else?" Work outward from there, asking, "Is this energy coming from my family, relatives, neighbors, friends, or co-workers?" Another way to uncover the source of bad vibes is to close your eyes and ask, "Who are you?" and then note who pops into your head. Next, ask, "What do you want?" and listen to the answer you receive.

Sometimes, no matter how hard we try, we can't be sure where negativity is coming from. The good news is that with practice, this will change. The more you train your mind to pay attention, the more psychically astute you'll become, especially when it comes to psychic protection. In the meantime, create a psychic shield of protection against negative vibes by saying, "Freeze!" and mean it.

My friend LuAnn taught me to take this even further by getting a glass jar with a lid and putting a piece of paper in it that says, "I freeze all negativity known or unknown moving toward me as of now." Fill the jar with water and blue food coloring for added protection, and actually freeze it. I once worked with a very unhappy assistant who continually projected her negative energy my way. I wanted to fire her, but I hadn't yet developed the confidence to do so, so I "froze" her instead. She quit the next day, and we were both relieved.

This practice always works miracles for me because as a ritual, it amplifies intention. Whenever you engage all your senses in an intention, it becomes very powerful. Hence, the glass, the food coloring, the writing, and the freezer all get my entire senses involved, including my imagination, which is the single greatest tool of intention we have.

You can also stop bad vibes by saying aloud to their source, "Take this back. I'm not willing to receive it. It's not mine." I say this every time I feel psychic barbs stabbing me in the back or in the heart. Sending energy back to its source like this keeps it from attaching to me, and lets the sender experience their own vibes so that they can make them positive.

<u>**Step #4.**</u> If you feel negativity coming your way from someone else, spiritual law instructs that you be loving and try to repair it. Negativity is often born out of misunderstandings that can be easily turned around if you approach someone with a loving and open heart. Bad vibes are often no more serious than bad breath, and they can be quickly cured. Find the offending problem, and cleanse it with loving communication. Say, "I feel confusion or negativity going on between us. Is there anything I've done to offend you, or is there anything you need from me that I am unaware of? I'd like to clear the energy between us, and I need your help." This creates a proactive, loving space in which everyone can express their unmet needs safely, and the energy will most definitely clear.

In fact, the best shield against negative energy is to surround yourself with lots of love and acceptance. This doesn't mean that you accept negativity, but you *do* accept that someone needs love, and bad vibes are just a very poor way to ask for that love. Forgiveness, compassion, and an open heart don't come easily to the psychic novice, or to people who prefer to see themselves as the victims. But as you embrace your vibes, this limited perspective will give way to a more creative and expansive view. As you psychically mature by giving up ego law and following spiritual law, you'll recognize that every event and experience in your life, good or bad, is an invitation for your soul to grow. If you're in doubt as to how to grow in a challenging energy, remember that applying love always works best.

<u>Step #5.</u> Finally, remind yourself that sometimes a bad vibe is just a bad vibe. Maybe someone's having a bad day (or a bad life), and you accidentally walked into their line of fire. I suggest that you not take anyone's negative energy personally, even if it *is* directed at you. Bad vibes are just missed opportunities to love, understand, and communicate effectively. So pray for healing— then use both feet and leave the area. As you do so, surround yourself with the most loving and kind thoughts possible. If you have any to spare, send the same caring thoughts to *all* approaching hostile forces—because they need it.

The simple act of distancing from negativity breaks the connection, clears the air, gets you grounded, and helps you drop your defenses. It opens your heart and leads you to a higher perspective. This is especially true when you find yourself in a heated argument. Leaving is best done with grace, sensitivity, and discretion. If you can quietly leave a toxic situation, get out as fast as you can. If the negative vibe is focused on you, but you can't leave easily or discreetly, simply say, "I need to walk and think. We can get back to this after we're both more grounded." Then go.

When you distance yourself, it helps to use your judgment wisely when it comes to where you go and with whom. If someone or someplace doesn't feel right to you, trust your vibes and stay away. Don't bother asking why something is off—you don't need to explain negative energy to know it's toxic. After all, when it comes to protecting yourself, you're in charge. No one else can do it better than you. Part of living a higher life involves paying attention to everything you feel and responding accordingly. Of course, this counsel assumes that you're not asking for bad vibes by following ego-based laws of disrespect and indifference to others' feelings. Doing this will attract the law of karma, or "What goes around comes around." The best defense is a good offense, so be as respectful and loving as possible to your fellow humans, even if you don't like them. And keep in mind that spiritual law says we're all connected, so who you're dealing with is only a reflection of *you*.

Six-Sensory Practice

This week, protect yourself energetically by consciously creating good vibes. Speak positively to yourself and others, and recognize who and what feels good. Pay close attention to the energy around you at all times. Remember not to take any negative vibration or energy personally—simply refuse to be harmed by someone else's missed opportunity to love. Shield yourself with positive, loving energy, and stop any unpleasant energy with intention. And know that if the vibes are really bad, you can always freeze them.

SIX-SENSORY WISDOM:

Call it like you feel it.

SECRET #10

TUNE IN

When you learn to trust your vibes, you'll break free of the illusion that we're only mortal and physical beings who are separate from one another and limited to physical space and time. You'll come to understand that, in fact, we exist in spiritual form, and whether our ego knows it or not, we frequently communicate with one another on an energetic level (which scientists call "nonlocalized"), sharing thoughts, feelings, ideas, and beliefs, as well as information.

We're also connected to every other soul on the planet through our heart center, which means that we have some form of conscious or unconscious telepathic rapport with others, near and far, as if we're sharing the same radio band. My teacher Dr. Tully said that most of us are in telepathic rapport with at least a thousand people at all times, and when particularly strong world events attract our attention, we can connect with up to *a million* souls at once, even if we're not conscious of it.

A common example of telepathic rapport is the kind that exists between family members. I remember when I was growing up, my mother only had to go out on the front porch and "think" us home to summon the family to supper. Since I've heard the same story from many of my clients, I believe that this is a fairly universal experience. I even wonder if "the power of Mom" is one of the strongest telepathic lines between people—after all, we come from our mothers, so this make sense.

The way telepathy ordinarily works is that we mentally tune in to the same vibratory frequency we send out, and we especially tune in the frequencies that we focus on or care about. It's a simple case of like attracting like: If we dwell on fear, focus on danger and injury, and feel like victims, we're going to draw the same to us. If, on the other hand, we focus on positive, life-affirming, and loving experiences, these will be returned to our field of consciousness by others.

I have a friend who's habitually negative and absolutely obsesses over how obnoxious, rude, and careless others are. Every time he turns on the radio, he inevitably hears a news account of another person gone mad. He's even found himself in the middle of outrageous outbreaks of rage more than once, such as on the highway when a woman tried to run him off the road, and in a movie theater when a couple nearly punched him out after he asked them to stop talking during the show. In fact, this guy has had more unpleasant encounters with strangers than anyone I've ever known. What's worse is that it doesn't end in his waking hours—he's also tormented in his dreams, having biweekly nightmares where shadowy figures are out to kill him. These energies are so powerful that he sometimes feels their presence in his room. He insists that negativity is taking over the world, which is true. But it isn't taking over *the* world, it's only taking over *his* world.

On the other hand, I know a man who refuses to dwell on or express anything negative as a matter of personal spiritual discipline. He contemplates peaceful thoughts and shares them wherever he goes. In return, he's the regular recipient of flowers, letters of appreciation, and small gifts; and generous, loving, and positive greetings from everyone he meets. He elicits the warmest responses from even the most cantankerous people. It's as if his telepathic broadcast is music to everyone's psychic ears, and he attracts the same warmth and affection from everyone around him. And not only does he succeed in keeping the frequency of his vibration powerful and very high, but the thoughts that flow into his field of awareness continue to be creative, humorous, and affectionate. He even receives profound messages in his dreams, which are filled with lovely images and beautiful music.

Sadly, these days most of us are like my pessimistic friend: We tend to be fascinated and even mesmerized by dark images. From violent movies and video games to even the nightly news, death and destruction seem to appeal to a worldwide audience that considers such things entertaining. Perhaps because a part of us feels dead and disconnected from life, this fascination with horror, violence, and evil images fills that void and in some perverted way makes us feel alive.

I'm not saying that a good horror or blow-'em-up flick isn't entertaining now and then, but feeding your psyche a steady and relentless diet of this type of entertainment is unwise. These images create fear, which leads to disease, depression, and despair—in a sense, becoming a telepathic cancer that eats away at our spirit. This is the worst form of psychic terrorism.

Unfortunately, negative frequencies have increased exponentially in the past 50 years due to radio, television, and the Internet. It's not that life itself is more negative, because there has never been more light and love on the planet than there is today. However, these mass-media and Internet broadcasts are manipulating the psychic airwaves, making it more of a challenge to avoid being sucked into the negative undertow. After all, you resonate with what you dwell on: If, for instance, you're a paranoid white supremacist who believes that the government is controlling the world, you'll attract all the other white supremacists who share your view, and soon you'll be channeling their mind-set along with your own.

The worst example in world history is that of Nazi Germany, where normally reasonable people were telepathically taken over and, in the process, went along with the idea of exterminating an entire race of people. It seemed that we'd eradicated this type of behavior, but we're now facing the same mass telepathic relay of destruction in radical Islamic terrorist groups. Again, we're seeing normally sane people turn into monsters. Just as there's mental indoctrination, there's also psychic indoctrination, so it's vitally important that a person who chooses to live according to spiritual law continue to fight this telepathic disease by sending out love to everyone all the time.

One way to prevent being telepathically hijacked is to keep your mind focused on what you love. The more you concentrate on what you care about and what feeds your spirit, the more you'll remain tuned in to the same positive telepathic counterparts in the psychic airwaves. And if you focus on uplifting, heart-based, and loving energies, you'll telepathically attract these vibrations into your life.

This is not merely some Pollyanna "stick your head in the sand" philosophy to avoid the real world, as those who are addicted to darkness and despair would suggest. No, this is a rebuttal to those who want to control us and have us submit to their negative projections. Mentally choosing to focus on love is a powerful weapon against the darkest of telepathic oppressors. Take, for example, Mohandas Gandhi, who liberated India telepathically by transmitting his unwavering conviction of peace. His focus was so powerful, and his broadcast to his fellow countrymen so grounded in love and nonviolence, that all of India united as one and gained their freedom without arms.

Each of us receives all sorts of telepathic telegrams every single day. Which ones will you accept? Those that broadcast and affirm vibrations of healing and light; or, like Chicken Little, those that create and communicate hysteria and darkness? Everything you dwell on adds to humanity's collective telepathic pool—while you may not be responsible for all the contamination out there, you *are* responsible for the pollution you personally add.

The greatest difference you can make in terms of healing the world is to telepathically send thoughts of healing and light as you simultaneously reject messages of darkness and despair. When you follow your heart, you become a beacon of light to others by broadcasting love and inspiration. And the more you convey light vibrations, the more they'll amplify, multiply, and return to you. Spiritual law says that you receive what you give times ten, so choose to put out a bright, loving energy to the world—in spite of appearances to the contrary, it *will* return. The more openhearted you are, the quicker the telepathic reception will be. Your heart chakra is the physical point in the body where telepathic signals are relayed back and forth, so you can attract the most remarkable of circumstances, opportunities, and encounters with others by intending to beam love. Here's an example of what I mean.

The license plate on my car broadcasts a personal message of good energy wherever I go. Ever since I installed it, driving in Chicago has transformed into a wonderful experience. People smile, wave, let me in, allow me to pass, give me parking spaces, and beam good vibes back to me. I love to get in my car now—it's an instant upper.

Telepathy is the most accessible of our six-sensory tools: Everyone is mentally talking to everyone else all the time, and everyone is tuning in. You're in telepathic chat rooms every second, whether you know it or not. If you pay attention to what crosses your mind, you'll see what I mean. So don't be a receptacle for psychic garbage by letting free-floating negativity take over your thoughts. Be vigilant and keep tuned to worthwhile, creative, and healing vibrations. And be responsible and send them out as well. As Dr. Tully said, "If you want to help the world, don't add to its problems."

Six-Sensory Practice

Pay special attention to what pops into your mind this week. Avoid dwelling on mental images that convey negative, depressing, violent, or destructive vibrations. This means turning off the television and radio and putting down the newspaper for the entire week. No matter what they report, if it's demoralizing and invokes fear, it doesn't serve you.

Zero in on what you say, and listen to it mentally. Recognize the correlation between what *you* broadcast and what comes back to you. What kinds of thoughts are you in the habit of thinking? Are you seized with fearful notions? Are you invaded by negative images? Do you receive jealous, angry, petty, inse-cure messages that drain you and leave you feeling unloved and unloving? If so, consciously change the channel. Mentally focus on higher things, and send out loving, peaceful messages to those around you. Envision your mind to be an FM radio station that receives and broadcasts high vibrations.

Read prayers and poetry; put down images of destruction and pick up art books; listen to classical music and positive con-versations; and turn your mind over to humor, laughter, and joyful music. Note the difference in the quality of thoughts that drift into your awareness as you mentally improve your airwaves. Also, see if what floats into your awareness adds to the quality of your life. It's really quite simple: If you want inspiration, think inspiring thoughts; if you want healing, think healing thoughts; if you want creativity, think creative thoughts; and if you want to live in a higher way, think higher thoughts.

SIX-SENSORY WISDOM:

Pay attention.

SECRET #11

GO WITH THE FLOW

If you want your vibes to guide you, then it's up to you to be as open to them as possible. One way to do so is to become flexible in your thinking and actions—in other words, go with the flow. As your sixth sense guides you from moment to moment, it will often suggest that you abandon your original plans and redirect your course of action quickly, without question or resistance. Spiritual law states that in order to live in a higher way, you should only make loose plans and be open to following all intuitive urges along the way. I can see why—you never know when spirit will need you.

This lesson hit home for me one snowy November afternoon several years ago. I was on my way to pick up my daughters from school, when, with one block to go, I suddenly felt an urge to drive in the opposite direction. Perplexed, but trusting that the Universe was at work, I turned around and followed still another impulse to turn left three blocks later. As I came to a stop sign, a toddler wearing only a diaper ran in front of my car and continued across the street. There was no adult in sight, so I parked the car and ran after her. Thankfully, I managed to grab the baby just before she was about to run through another intersection. *So this is the reason I had to drive away from school,* I thought, carrying her back to my car. *The Universe needed me to save this child.*

With the toddler tucked under my coat, I followed

my vibes, looking for signs of where she had come from. I was drawn to an open door, so I rang the bell. A young woman answered the door, and when she saw me standing with the child, she screamed, "Oh my God! Who are you, and what are you doing with that baby?" I explained what had happened, and she told me that she was only the child's babysitter. She said that she'd put the little girl down for a nap and was talking on the phone—she didn't even know that the baby was missing. I left the baby with her and then went to pick up my daughters (I was 35 minutes late). At first they were furious, but then they were happy when they learned I'd saved the little girl. (Later that night, I returned to the house to tell the mother what had happened in person.)

This story is a perfect example of the importance of being flexible. Had I resisted the impulse to turn the car in another direction, who knows what would have happened to that child? All I could think was, *Thank goodness I found her before she got hurt.* And because I was willing to be flexible and follow my vibes, the angels used me that day. In fact, the more flexible you are, the better of a candidate you become for your psychic sense to move through you and use you. My teacher Charlie once said that whenever he left the house he had notions about where he was headed, but he was never certain if he'd get there because Spirit might lead him elsewhere. I admired his willingness to follow his vibes, which led him to situations that blessed and graced his life every day.

Following his lead, I'm completely open to trusting my vibes and being flexible, especially when I travel. Of course I make plans, but I always leave them a little loose, just in case I'm led to something better. This kind of trust sends control freaks up the wall, but I find it incredibly exciting. It almost feels like a game I play with the Universe, and it has opened hundreds of doors for which I could never have prepared. For instance, on a trip to London, I waited to make a hotel reservation until the very last minute. I called a discount broker who said that he only had one room available for less than $100 a night, a bargain in London. Everyone had warned me of the difficulty of finding a reasonably priced, decent room in the city without an advance reservation, but I ignored them and trusted that it would work out.

When I arrived at the hotel, I was greeted politely by the desk clerk, who seemed perplexed when he looked up my reservation. He disappeared into the back room for several minutes, then returned and said, "I'm sorry, madam. We are overbooked. I just gave the last available room to the person before you. But don't worry—we're sending you to one of our other hotels where they can gladly accommodate you for the same rate."

"Would you mind telling me which hotel?" I inquired.

He smiled and said, "It's the Le Meridien Waldorf on the Strand, near Covent Garden. I think you'll approve, as it's the best location in London." In addition to giving me a five-star hotel room at the same rate, they sent me over in a taxi and even paid for it. My flexible, hang-loose approach had certainly paid off handsomely.

I recognize that as a seasoned intuitive who's quite comfortable going with the flow, this kind of blind trust may be a bit much if you're used to planning things in advance. I don't recommend that you be as daring or open as I am (although you'd probably enjoy it), but I do think that if you want to live in a higher way, it's necessary from time to time to leave room for your sixth sense to get in there and influence things. Then be sure to follow it when it does show up.

A CLIENT RECENTLY EXPERIMENTED WITH BEING FLEXIBLE when she wandered into a neighborhood that she'd always avoided. A few blocks into her walk, she happened upon an antique shop she hadn't known about. She found a beautiful old mirror that was the exact size and style she'd been searching for several months, at a price that was a steal. She was thrilled and grateful; now she makes it a habit to take an intuitively guided walk at least once a week in search of treasure.

A very good reason for listening to your vibes is to allow the Universe to lead you in the right direction. So, if you're a psychic Tin Man, stiff and inflexible, it's time to get out the mental oilcan and loosen up. Being flexible means giving up ego-based law, which says that you must know everything in advance, and following spiritual law, which says that you can be led to things along the way. The more you open your heart, and the more loose your attitude is, the more open to being guided you'll become.

I recently met a publicist named Bill at a reception for author Deepak Chopra, and I shared my views on how important a flexible attitude is to living the intuitive life. I explained my philosophy about being loose so that you can be guided moment to moment, and he told me that Phil Jackson, the ex-coach of the Chicago Bulls and current coach of the Los Angeles Lakers, agreed with me. "Don't watch [the other players'] heads, watch their hips," Jackson would tell the Bulls. "Their hips flow with the ball. That's how you'll know what's coming next."

People with rigid attitudes block the opportunity to let the Universe guide them. Who hasn't been a member of the woulda-shoulda-coulda club of missed opportunity simply because they were unwilling to make room for a better idea from the Universe? When this happens, you're reminded of the importance of following spiritual law because it brings opportunity, while ego-based law shuts it out. So the more you release your attachment to ideas about the way things have to be, the more your intuition can get in there and show you a better way. Now I'm not suggesting that you shouldn't set intentions or establish personal goals, because you absolutely must. Nor am I telling you to become an aimless wanderer, because that will only lead you in circles. What I'm advising is that you decide what you want, while at the same time leaving room for your Higher Self and the Universe to help you achieve it.

For example, my client Lucy lamented over her unwillingness to go into business with a high school buddy. Lucy had a goal to remain in her job five more years until she became eligible for early retirement, even though she loathed her job. "Everything in me said that I should quit and work with my friend in her software company," she said. "I loved the idea, I loved working with her, and I loved what she wanted me to do. My vibes were loud and clear, but my mind refused to trust them. I was so attached to my five-year plan, even though I hated my job, that I said no. Now, 18 months later, she's taking her company public and has earned millions. And here I sit, stuck in the same old familiar position, still hating my life. I really missed my chance, even though she offered it to me five times."

Sadly, Lucy missed her opportunity, as do most people who are unwilling to follow their gut. Yet a readiness to release plans and go with the feel of the moment is essential to six-sensory living. As one very successful client once told me, "I don't think— I feel. And I follow my feelings wherever they lead me. That's why I do so well."

How open are you to being spontaneous and following your intuition, even if it may mean changing plans? Do you tend to rigidly adhere to the same old routines and thoughts without ever allowing your intuitive genius to intercept and make a few suggestions? Are you so committed to sticking to the plan that you never allow your soul to lead? If so, you're following the rules of the ego, which as you know by now always leads to the same old predictable dead end.

Spiritual law reminds us that following your vibes is a lot like dancing. You may know the steps, but you won't succeed unless you're willing to move with the music. The Universe has a pulse and rhythm of its own, and it wants to carry you with it—so if you dance with Spirit, just remember to let it lead.

Six-Sensory Practice

This week, practice becoming more loose by doing some gentle bending and stretching before you start your day. Begin by raising your arms slowly over your head, gently rolling your neck, raising and lowering your shoulders, shifting your ribs, and rotating your wrists and ankles. Ease into this exercise, doing a little more stretching each day.

As I mentioned earlier, a good way to practice developing flexibility is to loosen your hips. An easy way to do this is to go in your closet and get out that hula hoop that's been slumbering there for a few decades (or maybe try your child's closet) and twirl it around for a few minutes. If you can't find a hula hoop, simulate the motion of the plastic circle revolving around your middle. (Remember how?)

Follow your physical-flexibility exercises with some mental-flexibility stretches. Invite your sixth sense to influence you by asking your spirit what it wants to do. If it wants to speak up, speak up; if it wants to be quiet, be quiet; if it wants to go on an adventure, go. Say yes to *all* your intuitive impulses, and be curious about where they'll lead you. Take a new route to work, wear something completely different from your usual outfit, consider a new pair of glasses, or get a new haircut, just for the sake of exploring a new you. Be curious, and surrender to your soul's lead by trying a new restaurant, exploring a hidden neighborhood, or going for an open-ended walk or a no-destination drive. Turn on some exciting music and dance—move, shake, twist, and bend just because you can. Better yet, dance with a blindfold on. (Just move the furniture first.) Don't worry—it isn't dangerous, only different.

One of my teachers once suggested that if I wanted to take full advantage of my sixth sense I had to act like Gumby, the pliable toy that can easily bend and stretch. If you have any children under the age of five, watch them for a couple of minutes and notice how flexible and spontaneous they are, not hesitating for a moment to change a plan, an idea, or a direction. Follow their example.

SIX-SENSORY WISDOM:

Be flexible.

SECRET #12

LIGHTEN UP

If you want to live a six-sensory life, you must clear away everything that prevents you from tuning in to higher vibrations—that is, everything that takes up space or energy but doesn't contribute to your life. This includes unnecessary and unwanted possessions, unfinished business, too many commitments, negative thinking, judgments, mental projections, resentments from the past, and negative associations in the present.

Let's start with your "stuff." Like psychic pollution, useless stuff creates dead, toxic energy that drags you down. As a six-sensory person, you must be vigilant in keeping your atmosphere alive and energizing, both internally and externally. Scrutinize everything in and around you, and ascertain whether these things add to or distract from your awareness. The clearer your space, the more you'll be able to keep the psychic airwaves of your life free of energetic obstructions and open to higher transmissions.

Just as you would never agree to spend time in a toxic-waste dump, neither should you agree to live or work in a psychically polluted atmosphere. Although you can't see dead energy, it still takes a toll—even seemingly harmless stuff can block good energy from entering your life.

An example of this occurred to me recently. I was looking for something to wear to a teaching engagement, and I tried on a dress that I hadn't worn for several years. Even though it was nice enough, it didn't feel quite right. My 12-year-old daughter, Sabrina, walked in, looked at me, and said, "Mom, you're not thinking of wearing that, are you?"

"Yes," I said. "Why not? It's a nice dress."

"It's okay, but it's not you."

She was absolutely right—this dress wasn't me. Even trying it on made me feel drab and lifeless, so I gave it away. You wouldn't think that simply giving away a dress could make much of a difference in the world, but it actually started a chain reaction that led to my clearing my entire closet of clothes that weren't the "real me" anymore. By the time I'd finished, I had emptied my closet of 12 bags of clothes! As I sent the last bag out the door, I was more inspired than ever and was back in the flow of life. I was suddenly more energized than I'd been in months, and I ended the writing slump I'd been in for a long time.

Clearing away dead energy restores the flow in your life and gets things moving in a higher direction. The Chinese art of feng shui is based solely on the principle of keeping your energy light and balanced so that your life flows freely. Now, just as you can "feng shui" your office or home, you can also "feng shui" your psychic atmosphere. If you pay attention to how things feel and what purpose they serve, you can get rid of anything that doesn't feel good or serve you. Be brutal—no matter how priceless an item may be, nothing is worth keeping if it doesn't give you a positive, light vibration, or if it distracts you from recognizing the subtle energy of the moment. Trust your intuition, not your intellect, when making these decisions, and let all your psychic sludge go.

Several years ago my sister gave my husband and me a Salvador Dalí painting that was quite valuable. We were both impressed and excited to own such a sophisticated piece of art . . . but the painting got on my nerves. Although Dalí is a great painter, the painting depressed me; nevertheless, for ten years I considered us lucky to have such a fine work of art in our home.

One day I looked at the painting and wanted to scream. In that moment, I knew the Dalí had to go, so I took it down and put it in the closet. That made me feel much better, but it wasn't enough—knowing that the painting sat in my closet still bothered me and took up too much of my attention. I thought about it every time I walked by that closet, as though it were being held hostage in the dark. Having had enough of this distracting energy, I finally sold the Dalí at a yard sale. I was so relieved to see it go that I couldn't believe I had kept it so long. I later sheepishly admitted to my sister what I'd done. She laughed and said, "I don't blame you. I hated that painting, too—that's why I gave it to you!"

Trusting your vibes means not only insisting on a clear space, but also keeping your environment as simple as possible so that energy isn't blocked or stuck in the past. Don't hold on to things for sentimental reasons or because "you might need it one day." This will just bog you down and cause you to miss the higher, lighter energies of spirit. Ruthlessly go through your stuff and get rid of everything that doesn't feel positive. And remember that as long as we hold on to things, they hold on to us.

I had a client, Lorraine, who experienced this firsthand. Lorraine's friend Gina was forever comparing herself to Lorraine, causing Lorraine to feel as though she needed to hide her successes and downplay the good things in her life for the sake of keeping Gina off her back. At first, Lorraine put up with it and even tried to compliment Gina as a way to even the field. Eventually, she could no longer tolerate Gina's negative energy and distanced herself from this unhappy, jealous woman.

While they were friends, Gina had given Lorraine a beautiful hand-painted Southwestern cross—but after they parted, every time Lorraine saw that cross she sensed the same unhappy energy she'd felt around Gina. As much as she appreciated the gift, Lorraine decided to give it away so that the energy could move on. She donated the cross to an auction at a Catholic school, which was delighted to have it. Lorraine felt relieved to have released the cross's burden. She never missed it.

A friend had a similar psychic revelation regarding an expensive coral necklace that her ex-boyfriend had given her. She'd had a very painful and unhealthy relationship with this man, yet everyone advised her to "keep the jewelry and forget the jerk"; if anything, he owed her that much. But psychically, it didn't work that way—even stuffed in her drawer, the necklace's vibrations left my friend sad, tormented, and unhappy. One day she opened the drawer and saw the necklace, and her spirit plummeted. "This is crazy," she said aloud, taking the necklace out of the drawer. "This thing is a downer." She realized that it caused her to feel drained and sad, and costly or not, she decided to move it out of her life. She put the necklace in her purse, and donated it to a nearby Salvation Army.

"It was like lifting a yoke off my shoulders," she told me later. Her heart instantly soared, and once out of the necklace's grip, she was even moved to have kind thoughts about her ex-boyfriend.

The importance of releasing old energy and keeping things light and simple can't be overstated. And it shouldn't be limited to the physical plane—we can become just as bogged down by old attitudes, negative thoughts and beliefs, heavy and melodramatic emotions, and even old relationships. These are the energy suckers that interfere with your ability to hear your Higher Self. Clearing out your *shtick* (as my 82-year-old Jewish friend, Ethel, calls it) may be more challenging than clearing your physical space, but it can be done.

In working with people one-on-one daily for nearly 35 years, I can unequivocally state that unless you remove this particular kind of psychic debris, your journey will most likely stop right here. In other words, you can't move one inch closer to trusting your vibes if you let your ego tenaciously cling to your hurt feelings, resentments, projections, frustrations, and angers without doing anything about it.

Be honest and humble enough to seek expert help to do this energetic clearing if you need it. The ego is too vain to admit that it needs anything, but spiritual law rejoices in gaining support. (Even Jesus Christ picked 12 helpers before he went to work. Maybe he was trying to tell us something.) So, if you're stuck, seek the help of healers, teachers, and guides of every sort. Clearing the past may require an entire team of assistants. You may need a 12-step group, *several* 12-step groups, a therapist, a support group, a massage therapist, a grief group, a church, a minister, a financial counselor, a coach, a personal trainer, an art teacher, a babysitter, an exercise buddy, *and* a new hairdresser.

Now most people would probably tell me that they can't afford this kind of support. But I say that if your life is being stolen and your spirit is dying, you can't afford *not* to seek help. Most services are free or at a reasonable cost. For example, 12-step meetings are free; community services offer counseling and support groups for as little as $10; massage-therapy schools are seeking bodies to work on all the time; teenage babysitters are always looking for work; and as for an exercise buddy, ask a friend. These services become affordable when you value them. Now if you value your misery more than your ability to live in your spirit, then, sadly, we'll probably part ways here—because no one and nothing, not even your psychic sense, can help you more than you're willing to help yourself.

I do not order you to "Get over it!" which is a popular approach by some military-style, self-appointed gurus to move people along. In working intimately with thousands of vulnerable, wounded, and overtaxed people for years and years, I've never seen this in-your-face method help heal anything. What does work, however, is for you to get *under* it, *through* it, *above* it, and *into* it until you learn how to love yourself and forgive other people. I believe in patience as we seek to dig out from under our "human experiences." No amount of yelling will work—but being determined to dig out will. You have to be self-examining and honest. Now I'll get off my soapbox and let that sink in. . . .

To sum up, if you want to reach out for something new, you must first let go of what's in your hand. Taking that even further, let go of what's in the closet, under the bed, and in your mind and emotions. Release your grip on anything that doesn't serve your spirit, and call in the troops for help. You need to free your attention to hear your sixth sense—if you're consumed with misery, you'll miss it. What's worth holding on to that would cost you that? Our planet can no longer afford to support those who insist on wallowing in the muck of old and negative vibrations. We're here to have a joyous life experience, not dwell on the dead past.

Six-Sensory Practice

This week, methodically clear out everything in your life that no longer uplifts your spirit. Start by emptying out your wallet or purse, and then move systematically outward through your desk, your car, your office, your closets and cupboards, your garage and your basement, or any other space where psychic trolls or dead energy may dwell. Keep nothing that doesn't leave you with a feeling of light, positive energy. Like a soldier protecting your kingdom, be ruthless in your assessment of whether or not you should keep something. And when you do eliminate it, be quick about it.

As soon as your physical space is clear, you'll have set the tone to address the energy suckers you host on a mental, emotional, or even psychic level. Take an inventory of where you're stuck, and don't get discouraged. Notice all the negative attitudes, resentments, dramas, and old vendettas you carry by writing them down (this may take you the entire week or even more).

Once you recognize how much psychic dead weight you carry around, take one step toward relieving yourself of it by seeking help. (If you don't know where to begin, read my book *True Balance*. It will help you identify the specific areas where you need aid, and it has an entire reference section for where to find that support.) If you have addictions, contact a 12-step group in your area—there are groups for those who abuse alcohol, drugs, money, and sex, as well as for those who live with or are in relationship with addicted people.

Perhaps you can use the support of a therapist, personal coach, or good six-sensory guide. Ask your doctor or your friends for a referral, and try several professionals until you find one who resonates with your soul. If you resist, remember that your ego is trying to keep you from becoming connected to your heart because it doesn't want to raise the quality of your life. And

know that while refusing to get support is death to your spirit, feeling scared is another thing. It's normal to be afraid to show your weaknesses and wounds to a stranger, but the minute you're around a true healer, this will end right away. Listen to your spirit and reach out. You aren't weak or broken—you're human, as we all are, and you need support, as we all do.

I know that seeking out soul supporters was the best decision I've ever made. They strengthened my ability to live in my heart, love my life, like who I am, and have compassion for the less enlightened. We're *all* students and teachers, and we need one another to learn.

Start small, but be diligent in your search for healing—and be patient. I know that clearing the past can feel like a huge and endless task at times, but even a few sessions with a talented healer or teacher, along with a focused effort, can free you considerably. At this point, the important thing is to decide to move on and not worry about how long it will take. The work of healing our past is called *karma,* and on a soul level, this work may take a lifetime or two, so don't rush it. Your peace won't begin *after* you heal, but *when you agree to* heal.

Green Fire

My favorite six-sensory ritual to open the way to a higher vibration on all levels is to make what I call green fire. Green fire cleanses the atmosphere, leaving it in a pristine state, and invites a fresh start. It's a powerful ritual to officially signal the beginning of a new season in your life. (Some five-sensory people think rituals are pagan and ridiculous—I prefer to see them as artful and creative, as they speak to our nonintellectual side. I've done rituals all my life, and I can absolutely assure you that they work.)

To perform a green-fire ritual, write down all that you desire to mentally and emotionally release. Next, grab some foil, a box of Epsom salt, a bottle of rubbing alcohol, a deep pot, and a match. Line the bottom of the pot with foil to protect it, fill it with two cups of Epsom salt, and pour enough rubbing alcohol over the salt to fully cover it. Place the pot on a protective plate in the middle of the floor of the main room of your home, apart from anything that can catch on fire. If you have a fireplace, put it there. As you light the mixture, ask your Higher Self, angels, and guides to help you release all old and negative vibrations, leaving your environment free and clear of any unwanted energy.

Place the list of old vibrations in the fire. It usually takes about 10 to 15 minutes for the fire to burn out, so remain with it. Whenever I burn green fire, I like to drum out the old energy as well. If you have a drum, you might want to do this; if you don't, you can always make one with another pot. Making loud noises helps dissipate negative energy as you burn the fire, so feel free to make loud sounds, grunts, or chants. Laughing is another great cleanser, and this ritual does makes one laugh. Another helper is to ring a bell while burning the fire. You can also shout at the energies in your home—a simple "Get out!" does the job, and it's fun to scream this.

A green-fire ritual is very powerful and effective and should only be done with real intention. I do it every three or four months, or whenever I feel a little blocked, just to clear and renew my spirit. It's a wonderful ritual to finish this week's psychic purge. Notice how much lighter and more conscious you feel after cleansing your energetic space.

SIX-SENSORY WISDOM:

This too shall pass.

SECRET #13

LET GO OF THE OLD STORY

As I've mentioned previously, six-sensory living requires us to raise our vibration enough to tune in to higher frequencies of energy. After all, Spirit is subtle and light, and if our energy is low, we'll miss it. Connecting to this loving, guiding force demands that we shift our mindfulness away from anything heavy, unloving, negative, dramatic, or fearful, for Divine Energy cannot infiltrate these thoughts or emotions.

Dwelling on the past is perhaps one of the greatest obstacles to Spirit. The more we focus on or even glamorize what happened to us yesterday, especially how unfair and unpleasant it was, the more we guarantee that we'll miss the subtle Divine Guidance being relayed to us at the moment. Sure, we all have a past, but interestingly enough, a big part of that story usually isn't our own—it's something we inherited from our parents.

For example, when people asked me who I was, I used to say that I was the daughter of a Holocaust survivor. Even though it was true, it was a very sad, restricting story that kept me defined by my mother's incredible misfortune and not by my own experiences. The more I focused on my mother's history, the less I was connected to who *I* was—to my path, my lesson, and my purpose. As glamorous, courageous, and romantic as her past was, I needed to let go and move into my own emerging story. I needed to look forward in my life, not backward at hers. The moment I made that decision, I released an incredible burden that wasn't just mine, it was my mom's as well. It freed us both energetically to discover the new story of who we are today and who we want to become tomorrow.

The liberation opened my healing heart, allowing me to hear my guides, feel my angels, and deeply understand those around me. By sharing this story with you, I don't mean to deny or minimize your personal history. I'm simply reminding you not to allow it to control or contain you, or keep you from growing into something greater. Our experiences, however fantastic or profound, never completely define who we are. Sure, they color our personalities and influence our perspective, but they're best used to learn from, after which they should be released.

When you let go of your past, your present truth emerges. It takes a lot of energy to carry your history with you all the time, and it clouds your connection to the Divine. So choose to become extremely curious about your new story, in what God has in mind for you now and for tomorrow. Then decide not to let your past define you anymore. Retire the old saga and move on.

If you slip, and find yourself looking backward, stop by saying, "That's the old story of me. Let's talk about the new one." Then do. See how your vibration lightens with this decision, and how much easier it is to hear your guides, spirit helpers, and angels. Look forward to being who you really are and to experiencing love, support, and even miracles in the process. Many things will distract you from Spirit; it's important to identify and eliminate them one at a time until you reach the point where Divine Guidance breaks through and gets your attention.

Six-Sensory Practice

This week, focus your attention and appreciation on your old story. If possible, write it down as thoroughly and dramatically as possible, and then share it with as many people as you can, telling it again and again. Observe how you embellish it each time

you tell it, and recognize the reactions you get. (If you can't find
sympathetic ears, tell it to yourself.)

Pay keen attention to any payoffs you get from replaying
this past drama. Do you feel sorry for yourself? Do you feel brave,
courageous, or heroic? Or do you feel small, crushed, or victimized? Notice how honest you feel each time you tell this story.
Does it accurately reflect who you are and who you want to be?
Do you feel light and loved? Blessed and loved by God? Guided
by your spirit helpers and angels?

After telling your story every day for a week, let it go. With
great respect and appreciation for all you've been through, decide
that it's time to release the past and step into the present.

SIX-SENSORY WISDOM:

Get a new story.

PART IV

Psychic Sit-Ups

SECRET #14

WRITE IT DOWN

Your vibes are useless if you don't trust them. Most people I've met *want* to trust their Higher Self, but they don't because they're afraid to. Over and over, I hear, "What if I make a mistake?" "What if my vibes are wrong?" or "What if something awful happens because my intuition is off?"

These are possible scenarios, of course, but they're highly unlikely. Trusting your vibes is a risk you'll eventually have to take if you want to grow into your own power. Standing on your own two psychic feet is a big and often scary decision, but it doesn't have to be the blind leap into the chaotic unknown that your ego will try to convince you it is. You can learn to trust your intuition in the same way you learn to trust anything else in life: through experience.

Your sixth sense invites you to partner with your Higher Self. And like any partnership, trust and confidence will develop naturally as you get to know one another. In other words, as you become more familiar with your spirit, the trust will evolve on its own.

The best way I know to begin this partnership is to get a small pocket notebook that you can carry with you at all times. Every time you get a hunch, gut feeling, "Aha!" moment, hit, sense, vibe, or any other input from your sixth sense, jot it down in your notebook. Don't let your ego censor, judge, discriminate, or in any way edit the information or feelings you receive. Don't worry if your vibes feel silly, irrelevant, irrational, or stupid; or if you think that what you feel is nothing more than your imagination. Write it all down anyway. Your mind will see that every vibe you have makes sense in one way or another over time.

You won't have to trust *me;* you'll have the evidence. As I tell my students, if you record your vibes faithfully for three weeks, all your doubts will start to shrink and give way to growing confidence because you will have collected solid evidence that your sixth sense is worth trusting.

Sadly, many of my clients and students are unable to even recognize, let alone name, their intuitive feelings with accuracy because they habitually "stuff them." Writing vibes down will cure this. For example, my student Barry said, "I used to automatically strangle my vibes before I knew what they were. If I felt uneasy, rather than take my hunch as a warning, I'd go in the opposite direction immediately, telling myself that I was crazy—everything was fine.

"Inevitably, my uneasiness would turn out to be accurate, but because I ignored it, I'd have even more problems. Once I began writing down my intuitive flashes, however, I relaxed and was able to start discovering exactly what my intuition had to say. To my surprise, a lot of it made sense."

My client Kyle told me that recording his vibes was simply good practice: "The more I wrote, the more vibes I noticed. Soon it occurred to me that I was actually getting hits that I regularly ignored until I began my journal. And they were accurate."

Another client, Louise, reported, "I started noting my vibes in general, but soon they started to focus on specific things such as the stock market. This had been a hobby of mine, but never something I allowed myself to take seriously. My stock predictions were on-target for three weeks. I didn't invest any money, but I sure wish I had!"

Recording your vibes is the most direct physical way to march your mind across the bridge from an ego-based, five-sensory reality to a spirit-based, six-sensory one. Like a diver on a treasure hunt, each newly seized message from your psychic sense will help build a platform of reason on which to stand. You'll no longer just have a feeling—you'll have verification that your vibes are legitimate guides that help your life.

Keeping a journal also directs your subconscious mind to acknowledge that your intuition is important, which for most people is a revelation. Every time you write something down, you verify that it's worth noting, even if it doesn't make sense that moment. It won't take long for your subconscious to get the message and to cooperate even more.

If you've trained yourself to ignore your sixth sense, recording your vibes will "untrain" you—that is, your intention will be restored to a proper place of importance, and gives you back this necessary part of yourself. Fortunately, our higher channel is amazingly resilient, and with a minimal amount of effort, it will bounce back into action, even after a lifetime of being ignored. Your intuition is natural and an integral part of who you are as a soulful being—it's *unnatural* to be so disconnected from your vibes that you don't trust or even feel them.

The best reason of all for keeping a six-sensory journal is because it's fun. There's something inherently reassuring in knowing that behind the scenes you have help. You aren't just making it up to feel better—there really are higher forces at work on your behalf, and they're doing a great job. Even your ego will be impressed by a psychic journal because the evidence will be undisputable. It will actually begin to take pride in being so intuitive, and you will seriously advance. After all, your ego isn't the enemy— it really is trying to help you, although it isn't capable of doing a very good job. So don't kill it, just prevent it from being the final word. The idea is for your ego to give way to your intuition, which is smarter and better equipped to live in a higher way.

With each journal notation, your six-sensory radar will get sharper and more accurate and entertaining. It's very empowering to look back at what you've written and realize how brilliant your sixth sense really is. Each entry, like a newly discovered pearl of wisdom, will have great value, if for nothing else than to remind you of how magnificent your artful soul really is.

Six-Sensory Practice

I find it best to have two journals: one for the road, and one that you keep at home. The one for the road can be small, while the one at home can be more substantial.

Carry the little one with you everywhere, and record everything your vibes relay to you. If you hate writing, you can modernize this practice by using a handheld organizer or a small pocket tape recorder. Speak freely; record every vibe you have and don't censor yourself. You never know if something that doesn't make sense now will have meaning later.

SIX-SENSORY WISDOM:

Make a note of it.

SECRET #15

The hotline that connects you to your Higher Self is prayer, which is simply the practice of communicating on an intimate, heart-to-heart level with your Creator. When you pray, you ask your ego to step aside, and you surrender your personal energy to a Higher Power. Prayer is basic training for anyone who wants to stay faithful to their intuitive voice and live in a higher way. It not only opens you up to receiving assistance from a Higher Power, it also relieves you of the stress of figuring things out for yourself. And one of the hallmarks of a six-sensory being is the absence of worry over how things will work out. Prayer involves simply leaving it up to God.

Prayer immediately raises your personal vibration, ushers more light into your body, and opens your heart center—all of which activate your sixth sense and connect you with your spirit. In study after study, research has shown that prayer has a healing effect on the physical and emotional body, calming anxieties, soothing nerves, and easing tension. It has even been known to relieve high blood pressure, lift depression, and cure sickness. As it heals, calms, strengthens, balances, and restores order, prayer also attracts solutions that we could never imagine were possible—in other words, miracles.

There's no one way to pray. Since it's such an intimate connection with Spirit, the right way is however you intuitively feel moved to do so. For example, I know people who wouldn't dream of beginning a day without reciting the rosary aloud, while others kneel in devout silence. I have friends who pray by going for a walk, while others go to a synagogue, mosque, or church. Some people I know pray formally, while others simply chat with God in their minds. I have neighbors who gather together in a religious ceremony like the Sabbath, while others commune in drum circles, chanting, dancing, and even sweating. I pray in all these ways and more—in fact, from the time I open my eyes until I fall asleep, I'm praying, because I don't like being disconnected from God.

The other day I logged on to the Internet, and much to my dismay, something was wrong with my computer, so I couldn't establish the connection I wanted. I felt frustrated at being unable to gain access to this vast and free resource when I really needed to. Well, praying is very similar to logging on to the Internet, only better. When you pray, you spiritually log on to Divine Wisdom, which is the ultimate resource for support and guidance.

I often ask people if they pray. Almost everyone answers that they do, but when I ask how often, they tell me "now and then," or "in an emergency." These individuals all have various reasons for not praying, and some are even rather noble. Some say they don't want to bother God, others claim that they save their prayers for important matters, but most often, people have told me that they don't pray simply because they forget to.

Like everything else that connects us to our Higher Self, prayer is most effective when practiced, meaning that you should pray *whenever* you think of it until it becomes automatic. In other words, pray when you wake up in the morning, while you take a shower, before your drink your morning coffee, and as you drive to work. Pray for the easiest and best way to get through your day. Pray for success in your projects and for patience when those around you get on your nerves. Pray for forgiveness and an open heart. Pray for creative inspiration and for better health; to release the past and to open your mind and heart to a better future; for the willingness to let go of the old and outdated and reach out for something new; for understanding;

for faith; for a happy heart, in spite of everything; for the right support system and the best job; and for a peaceful home and prosperity.

These are just some suggestions to get you started. You get the idea—you can (and should) pray for everything and everyone you can think of.

WHEN I WAS IN THE FIFTH GRADE, my teacher, Sister Mary Joan of Arc, had us create a personal collection of our favorite prayers. I loved my first homemade prayer book, and I've been making them ever since. Every time I read or hear a prayer that I love, or that speaks to me in some meaningful way, I write it in my prayer book; and I've also included devotions that I've written myself. My prayer book has become a tremendously important and intimate part of my spiritual and intuitive practice and support system. It has such a beautiful vibration that simply holding it brings me a deep sense of peace and inner tranquility—it feels holy, and it is. Just having my prayer book near me serves as a great source of inspiration and protection, so I take it wherever I go.

Even though I've kept a personal prayer book for more than 30 years, I've rarely mentioned it to anyone else. Lately, however, I've felt a need to tell others about this powerful tool so that they can create one for themselves. Look at the popularity of Bruce Wilkinson's book *The Prayer of Jabez*—if a prayer as impersonal as one written by someone you've never heard of can be so powerful, can you imagine how potent a book of personal, familiar, intimate, and treasured prayers could be? The intentions within such a book will take on a grace and power of their own as they're accumulated over the years, and I assure you, the vibration is extremely powerful.

Several of my loved ones also keep prayer books. For example, my friends LuAnn and Joan both have a collection of special devotions to Mother Mary, while my mother has a collection of prayers that she uses to ask for miracles—and it has come in very handy. You see, one of my mother's clients once gave birth to a baby boy who was born brain-dead—the woman was nearly hysterical, and the entire family was devastated.

My mother went to her prayer book and began to pray for this child even though he was placed on life support and wasn't given a chance to live. A week later, the doctors suggested that the child be removed from life support so that nature could take its course. All the while, my mother prayed for a miracle and didn't allow herself to consider anything less. The baby was unhooked and expected to die; instead, he took a big breath and lived. And to everyone's amazement, he suffered no brain damage. A year later, he was even the subject of a *Denver Post* story called "The Miracle Baby." Does prayer work? I'd say yes, without question.

Whenever I'm asked how we know if our prayers are heard, I always answer, "By the peace of mind that follows." For example, I've known my client Susan for more than ten years. I've watched her struggle with finding and keeping job after job as a writer for television, as well as searching for the perfect partner and harmonious family relationships. No matter how much I assured her that all would be well, she never believed me.

Finally, I suggested that instead of trying to control everything, she seek to heal her fear and anxiety by praying. I could psychically see that her vibration was resonating at an extremely negative level in the company of everyone looking for work in Hollywood. This search, driven by fear and survival, was draining the life force out of her. By praying, she could shift the energy to a higher level and get some immediate relief.

She reacted to my suggestion by laughing. When I asked her why she responded in this way, she answered, "Because my mother was a religious fanatic, and she always forced prayer on me. I rebelled and haven't prayed since I left home at 17. It just sounds so odd to me to pray."

"Did praying help your mother?" I inquired.

Susan was quiet for a moment, and then said, "You know, I'd have to say that it did. When I was growing up, we went through some tough times, yet she always managed to pull through, saying that it was prayer that saved her. Maybe she was right."

By the time our conversation ended, Susan was feeling much better. Simply thinking about praying helped ease her anxiety, and she had yet to begin. That's how powerful prayer is.

Prayer also prepares me for my psychic readings. I use the same ones every time: (1) "Divine Father, Holy Mother, use me," (2) "God, please take this out of my hands and place it in yours," and (3) "Thank You." All three make my life very simple because they allow me to be open and receptive to Divine direction, and they offer up my appreciation for my gifts as well.

I don't suggest that you follow any "rules of praying"; instead, just pray when you feel like it, about anything you feel like, and in whatever way you feel like. Don't worry if you're doing it right—God knows better than you what you mean and need. The point is not so much what you pray for or how you pray, but that in praying you allow the Divine Spirit to enter your heart. The beauty of prayer is that with it, God straightens things out and always better than we could have asked for or imagined. So pray to strengthen your intuition and help you expand into a more soulful, guided, six-sensory, artful being. And if your psychic workout relies heavily on prayer, you'll immediately feel the expansion in your own consciousness, as well as the relief and the peace of mind prayer can bring.

Six-Sensory Practice

Every day this week, pray the instant you wake up. You may want to start by thanking your Creator for giving you another day on this beautiful planet; or if you have any pressing concerns, ask for assistance and protection and for blessings throughout the day. During the day, pray whenever you think of it. Pray for your family, friends, neighbors, and co-workers. Pray for your enemies, and pray for the world. Pray for everything that concerns you, for all that gives you reason to doubt. And pray in gratitude for all your blessings. Pray to remember to pray.

Creating Your Personal Prayer Book

Why not create a prayer book of your own? Begin by selecting an attractive journal with blank pages, then simply write down all the prayers you hear, read, or write yourself that bring you peace, speak to your heart and soul, and uplift your spirit in any way. Because ritual is such an important part of many prayers, you may want to integrate it into your prayer book by writing with a specific pen, one that makes the entries especially meaningful and sacred.

You might also want to print your prayers in a distinctive manner—perhaps you'll feel moved to draw something sacred or place a holy card or talisman in your book for inspiration. This is *your* personal collection, so trust your spirit to move you to create your prayer book in whatever way speaks to you best.

I carry my prayer book with me all the time, especially when I travel. I suggest that you do the same, even taking it to work with you. Who knows, this might be exactly the place where you'll need it most. Creating your own prayer book is a beautiful way to develop the practice of prayer and the habit of keeping your heart open to spiritual guidance—which is the way of the six-sensory being. Just having it in your possession will be healing.

SIX-SENSORY WISDOM:

Pray.

SECRET #16

It goes without saying that activating your sixth sense will make you more sensitive. Sounds will amplify, everything you touch will take on an exaggerated feel, what you see may affect you in a much more profound way, and you may even develop a super sense of smell—all because your psychic channel elevates your awareness of your energy body, called the *aura*.

Your aura is the energy field that surrounds your physical body, and it's usually up to 12 layers in thickness. As any professional intuitive will attest, when your aura is sensitized, *all* your senses go up an octave to perceive energy in the fourth dimension. This means that your vision may expand to the higher octave of *clairvoyance*, your hearing may expand to the higher octave of *clairaudience*, and your sense of touch may expand to the higher octave of *clairsentience*—or the three basic six-sensory channels. (Your sense of smell may also become more acute, and although there's no specific term for it, you may get "a nose for things.")

Like setting up a satellite dish on the roof, the result of this expansion is that a lot more energy floods through your senses as more awareness comes in. The result can be quite overwhelming in the early stages. For example, one woman told me that her intuitive awakening "was like nuclear power suddenly coursing through a toaster."

She was left feeling fried, especially when she was in very loud, intense situations.

"Things that didn't bother me before do now," said my student John. "It's like I've just woken up. For instance, suddenly I can no longer go to bars. I just can't stand the noise, the smoke, and the feeling."

Carmen, another student, explained, "I've always been sensitive to what I heard, but after I began to use my sixth sense, I found that I couldn't listen to office gossip anymore. I wasn't taking a moral high ground—I just couldn't stand the way it made me feel."

As your sixth sense opens more, you'll become more sensitive to the quality of vibrations around you and their effects, which is a part of being psychic. Living a six-sensory life compels you to be more selective about what you tune in, just as you would be when watching satellite TV. In other words, just because you can pick it up doesn't mean that you'd want to watch it.

"The more my sixth sense opened up," said my client Donna, "the more I felt on a deeper level what was true and what wasn't. It's hard to explain, but I could tell by how it rang, or resonated in my head, when people told me the truth. When they lied, it felt like a sour note that made my ears hurt."

I once worked with Detective JJ Bittenbinder, who had a show in Chicago called *Tough Target* in which he taught people to use their vibes for protection. He called his sixth sense his "bs sensor." In other words, each and every one of us has an inner psychic-truth barometer that guides us and, once activated, takes on the perception of radar. As my client Adam told me, "After taking your intuition class, it became really annoying to listen to someone lying to me because my own bs sensor sounded off like an alarm." I knew what he meant. It can be almost painful to your intuitive ears to hear someone lie—it's often so internally loud that it feels as though that person is running their nails across a blackboard.

As your vibes fine-tune, you may also have an overwhelming craving for silence because you're unconsciously trying to regulate the rush of vibration as it pulses through your aura. Your attention is shifting away from the physical world and your ego;

instead, you're turning inward and upward toward your Higher Self. Unless you have enough internal silence, you won't be able to hear your inner voice or your guides, so the yearning for silence is a sign that your natural channel is opening to spiritual assistance. This explains why mystics are usually in or seeking silence—it connects them to God.

"I'm so desperate for quiet," said a client, "that sometimes I run to the garage and sit in my car for ten minutes. With three boys under the age of five, that's the only place I can find some peace. I can't wait to do this every afternoon."

As you begin to open your own sixth sense, you may also develop a strong reaction to what you see. As your sensitivity to vibration increases, so too will your need for beauty. And if you don't get exposed to enough of the earth's loveliness, you'll probably start to crave it. I found that the more sensitive I became over the years, the more I needed to get out of the city and into the country to soothe my nerves and shake the energy of my clients out of my aura. A student of mine realized a similar craving for beauty, but it manifested in a different way: "Suddenly, all I wanted to do was paint," he told me. "I spent hours and hours doing watercolors, and the more I did it, the more it fed my soul."

How we connect to beauty is up to our individual nature, but most people who expand into higher awareness say it feels necessary. For example, Steve, a Chicago Police Department detective who spent all his time dismantling street gangs, was rapidly awakening his sixth sense and noticed that it was affecting him quite a bit. "My work demanded that I use my nose for trouble," he said, "and eventually it seemed that my nose for other things kicked in, too. I began to have a sixth sense about everything, so I took your class to develop it. A funny thing happened after that—all I wanted to do was visit museums, something I'd never even thought of before. My buddies laughed at me, saying I was going fancy on them, but now I have a few of them going with me, and they see what I mean."

Once your intuitive sensibilities wake up, it becomes very difficult to expose yourself to things that disturb the spirit, such as violence, chaos, and even too much concrete. If you do become overexposed, you'll instantly start to gravitate toward more healing things and places. The ego numbs our senses, so when our sixth sense wakes up, so do our sensibilities. We realize that we need harmony and beauty and can't tolerate gross violence on a gratuitous level because it's dissonant to our spirit.

The soul's need for beauty has affected my clients in different ways. When Larry awakened his Higher Self, he started reacting to things he once paid no attention to, such as the graffiti in his neighborhood. He organized a massive community graffiti-busting campaign because he couldn't stand the vibration it emitted.

As she awakened her sixth sense, my client Linda could no longer watch violent TV shows or movies. "Until now, I thought it didn't affect me," she said. "I'm stunned that I didn't realize it did—because now when I see this kind of stuff, my energy immediately drains out of my body. I don't want to regulate TV or movies; I just regulate what *I* watch because it affects me. It's as though the volume has been turned up, and now I'm aware that I'm being bombarded with vibes. I'm careful to be more selective about which ones I can control."

As you move toward a six-sensory life, you'll become aware of how delicate and sensitive a soul you are. And the more you evolve, the more you'll recognize what upsets your internal psychic equilibrium. As Louis explained, "Before I started listening to my Higher Self, I was very careless and sloppy in what I wore, often grabbing any old thing and not really caring how I looked. But after I began to live in a six-sensory life, I became very picky about what I put on. It's not a fashion thing, either—it's an energy thing. Once I began feeling things on an intuitive level, I no longer wanted to wear certain fabrics like polyester, because the vibes were uncomfortable. I wanted clothes made of natural fibers, which felt good on my skin and comforted me."

Tom said, "After I started to pay attention to my vibes, I couldn't wear a tie anymore. It just wasn't me, and I couldn't stand it. I had to take it off! Thank God my work didn't require me to wear one, because the vibration was too restricting."

Another client noted, "Once I started to listen to my intuition, I couldn't wear dark colors—they were too depressing. I wore only white or pastels, and I felt much better. It just felt necessary to my soul."

Bob, one of my regular students, said the opposite: "Suddenly I craved wearing dark greens and browns—and no more suits. I had to have sweaters because they felt right. They calmed me."

Don't worry—awakening your intuitive center won't make you eccentric, suddenly needing the right shoe, the right fabric, and the right color. It simply makes you more discerning and self-aware. You've always needed beauty; nature; solitude; balance; and harmonious sounds, sights, and textures—but now you'll realize that without such things, you're diminished.

Living a six-sensory life does make you more sensitive, however, which is why psychics and intuitives are called *sensitives*. As you become more psychically aware and more faithful to spiritual law, your choices will shift more to respecting and preserving your inner peace—recognizing where you are, with whom, what you're doing, and what it's doing to you. You'll be able to honestly determine whether or not what's happening feels good—if it doesn't, you'll be brave enough to step away even if it feels awkward (five-sensory people will think you're being too fussy).

Being more energetically discerning may cause concern that it will make you look like a pristine "wuss," as one of my clients, Josie, called it. Yet I've observed that ignoring what the spirit needs is what's exhausting, not the opposite. As for being a wuss, well, maybe you are, but so what? Rather than worry about or hide the wuss in you, change your attitude and realize that your inner wuss is actually your sensitive soul. So don't resent it, appreciate it. As an intuitive, I can tell you that your inner wuss's real name is "self-love."

So, in the name of self-love, listen to your vibes. Many of my students have testified that before they listened to their vibes they mindlessly committed to anyone at any time without checking in with their sixth sense, but since becoming psychically sensitized, their priorities have changed dramatically. So if something is calling you, don't hesitate to follow it. If something offends you, distance yourself from it. Visit nature if it calls you. Settle down. Go within. And trust your vibes.

Six-Sensory Practice

This week, listen to what your senses tell you and what they ask for. Pay attention to your environment and the sights, sounds, and feel of those things in it. If you feel a dissonant energy or vibration, or if something feels like a downer, tune it out, turn it off, or move away. Start with your clothing—as you get dressed, from your underwear out, notice if your clothes feel good on your skin or if they raise your vibration. If something you're wearing doesn't feel good, change it fast.

Also, keep your nose sharp. If something doesn't smell right, don't ask questions, just trust the message you're receiving. Be aware of smells and how they affect you. Try adding aromatherapy, scented candles, perfumes, and incense and see if they raise or lower your vibration. And take the time to give all your senses a break. Sit in silence in a quiet, dark space, and rest. Then listen for your guides, and focus inward.

SIX-SENSORY WISDOM:

Be sensitive.

PART V

Creating a Six-Sensory Support System

SECRET #17

REMEMBER, IT'S A TEAM EFFORT

Y ou won't trust your vibes if you have to hide them, so you need to share with kindred spirits to gain your confidence. One of the most frequent comments I hear from clients is, "I wish I had your gift and could listen to my sixth sense like you do. It would make my life so much easier."

True, I do have a gift—in fact, I have several. But I'm probably most grateful for my psychic soul mates, who, like me, are six-sensory beings who talk to Spirit, are aware of life on the Other Side, and listen to their vibes. Being surrounded by such loving and believing eyes and ears has made being psychic much easier than if I were alone.

I was very fortunate to grow up in a home where my sixth sense was accepted and encouraged, and I was allowed to express and develop it without any danger of ever being laughed at or dismissed as crazy. It was also wonderful to have a six-sensory mother who set the tone in our home, enabling me to explore my psychic capabilities freely without censorship and in a spirit of creativity and play. Not only did my mother encourage me to recognize and respect my intuitive vibes, but my brothers and sisters were also great sounding boards when I wanted to practice expressing my sixth sense without being self-conscious or doubtful.

I honed my six-sensory skills at home the way other kids practiced the piano. I shared my vibes every day, as if I were playing psychic scales. Sometimes my vibes were sharp, while other times they were off—but with daily practice, they got more acute, more consistent, and more reliable. I'm certain that this atmosphere was the very incubator I needed for my sixth sense to develop into the powerful guiding force it is for me today. Without this practice at home, I never would have gained the confidence or good habits I needed to listen to and trust my inner voice the way I do now. Sharing my sixth sense with my family strengthened my inner voice until it became more and more comfortable for me to use as a primary compass in my life.

Many of my clients and students have told me that their experiences concerning practicing their sixth sense made it difficult or nearly impossible for them to express their intuitive feelings safely and with support. These stories merely affirm my conviction that being surrounded by kindred spirits is essential to a six-sensory life. All the intuitive people I know hang out with at least one or two other six-sensory individuals, for being free to express your psychic sense to interested and accepting people is fundamental to opening your intuitive channel. Those who, like me, grew up with positive reinforcement are much more at ease with their psychic voice than those who have had only five-sensory people to relate to.

I've heard countless horror stories over the years from people who grew up in a five-sensory world where they wouldn't have dared to openly express or share their intuitive feelings for fear of being censored, laughed at, or perceived as crazy. If that was the atmosphere you were exposed to, it doesn't have to be that way now. You can expand your options today and start to create a much safer, receptive sounding board to bounce things off of. You can give your sixth sense some legs by seeking kindred spirits.

First, you must recognize that you need a grounded and interested six-sensory support system with which to share your psychic vibes. It's easy to believe that you're "the Lone Ranger in psychic land" (as a favorite client calls it)—that is, if you let anyone know about your gifts, they'll shoot you on sight. However, the New-Age industry is one of the largest moneymakers in

America, selling billions of dollars worth of books, tapes, and seminars on the sixth sense and related spiritual pursuits every year. If you think that you're the only person with these interests, then you probably haven't been to a bookstore lately.

In reality, *millions* of people are in six-sensory land, but they're hiding for fear of ridicule. I believe that almost everyone these days is in the psychic closet to some degree, so it must be getting pretty crowded in there. If you "step out of the closet" and reveal your interests to others a little more—or at least turn on the light and see how many other people are secretly pursuing spiritual and intuitive growth these days—you'll be on your way to finding lots of support from the most unexpected places.

When I do public workshops and readings, people show up in the hundreds, and many of them claim to be skeptics—yet they can't help but ask questions or seek some guidance from me. For example, I once read for Carl, who said that he thought he had a few vibes, but he lamented over his lack of psychic support, especially at work. "I'm six-sensory and sensitive," he said, "but I work with Neanderthals who are so insensitive and unconscious that it's scary. I wouldn't dare let them know my interests, or they'd laugh me out of the office."

I invited Carl to a workshop so that he could meet other "six-sensory team players." He was stunned to see several of his co-workers there—but I wasn't. After all, we tend to presume to know what others are like, and we're often wrong. It's best to keep an open mind and assume nothing as we seek psychic support. In the Dark Ages, six-sensory people *did* have to hide and sneak around for fear of being misunderstood and attacked. Fortunately, people have slowly evolved over time, so this is becoming less and less of a problem. Of course, some people still don't get it, but happily, more and more are starting to.

If you feel that you can strengthen your vibes on your own without any support, you're kidding yourself. Even intuitives need supportive people to help us remain true to ourselves, especially when it comes to trusting our vibes. So actively seek out your soul supporters (those other six-sensory people who are embracing spiritual law) as part of your effort to open your psychic channel. Find people you can connect with, who will listen to you, and who will respect your vibes and keep them safe and protected from negative judgment, including your own—in other words, your team. These people do exist, and you need to connect with and put them in your life as fast as possible, for six-sensory people are most comfortable in tribes—we don't do as well alone. As I said earlier, even Jesus Christ picked 12 helpers before he went to work. Let's use him as a role model and begin to seek our own supporting cast.

When seeking support, don't let your ego sabotage you by confiding your intuitive feelings to those who clearly aren't supportive. Be discerning when sharing your vibes or seeking soul supporters. If you go to another six-sensory person, or at least another person interested in psychic matters, you'll be fine—but if you confide in someone who's still unaware of their soul, you'll set yourself up for failure.

Exercise a little common sense here. You probably already know that five-sensory people don't get it and are often dismissive and discouraging when it comes to vibes, so do your detective work first. For example, when I was a teenager I had a good friend named Vicky. An only child of a single parent, Vicky had an extremely sharp sixth sense and frequently had very accurate vibes. Yet every time she shared her vibes with her five-sensory (and superstitious) mother, she'd get flustered and say, "Stop, Vicky! You're scaring me." This reaction frustrated my friend because she wanted her mother to listen to and appreciate her insights and not shut her down.

Once, the three of us were in a car together when Vicky suddenly said, "Mom, slow down. I feel that a cop is in the area, and you're speeding." As always, her hopelessly five-sensory mother overreacted: "Vicky, don't say things like that. You sound weird." And she didn't slow down.

Two blocks later, a cop pulled out of the shadows, flagged down Vicky's mom, and gave her a ticket for speeding. But rather than admit that she'd made a mistake, Vicky's mom blamed *her* for the ticket. I couldn't believe it, and neither could Vicky. It made no sense. I later mentioned to Vicky that maybe she shouldn't share her vibes so freely with her mom because this woman was so trapped and scared by her ego that she didn't understand vibes, and she never would. Instead, I suggested that Vicky share her vibes with *my* family because we'd be far more receptive.

From that day on, Vicky stopped sharing her vibes with her mom, and she adopted my family as her psychic team. The more we listened, the more comfortable she became as a six-sensory person, and the more fun she had. By the time Vicky entered college, her sixth sense was her main barometer—she even used it for guiding others by doing intuitive readings. I believe that she developed her six-sensory skills because she had so much support from us as her team.

Unlike Vicky, if you look into your own family, chances are good that you may find at least one ally. It's worth the effort, because family support is the best there is. But look for those who've already shown interest; under no circumstances seek to recruit someone you have to work to persuade. We all awaken to higher awareness at our own pace, and no one can hurry anyone else along. If a five-sensory person doesn't get it, move on. Seek support, not sabotage.

If there's no one you can go to at home, see if anyone at work shares your interests. You can test the waters by asking your co-workers if they listen to or believe in intuition. I know this seems scary, but don't assume the worst—intuition is an exciting and intriguing subject for many people these days. I know that work isn't the best place to look, but since you go there every day, it's worth a peek because it would be convenient if you're successful.

If you can't find team players at home or at work, see if any friends or neighbors share your interest. Raise the subject of intuition casually and see what happens. It's my experience that those who are interested are *really* interested and love to share, so it won't take much to get them out of the psychic closet. You can also find team players in places where they tend to congregate, such as workshops, lectures, or progressive churches where following your psychic sense is encouraged and supported.

All you really need is one or two sympathetic playmates to talk to from time to time. That's all. I'm not advising you to join a cult or an exclusive, secretive, or controlling group. That's not support—that's creepy, so please stay away.

Once you *do* find your six-sensory team members, check in with them often, for at least a few minutes a week. Encourage the people in your group to freely share, and respectfully listen to one another's intuitive feelings without doing anything about it. Just listen—that's the best support anyone can give or receive.

One final note: I've found that one of the quickest and most efficient ways to find your team is to simply pray for them to show up. Ask God to connect you with the best six-sensory partners you can have, and He will. Your job is to cast the psychic fishing line and find your team. It isn't as hard as you think. When you're ready and willing to receive support, it *will* show up, and usually quite easily.

Six-Sensory Practice

This week, look for your team players. Maybe you have a few already—if so, establish check-in times with them when you can share your vibes. If you aren't sure who your fellow team players are, do a little detective work and flush them out. Use this book: Lay it on your coffee table or desk, and observe the reactions it receives. If someone shows interest in the subject of intuition and vibes, explore a little further. It won't take long to discover whether you've found someone who can be supportive. On the other hand, if someone is disinterested, don't take it personally—they simply aren't ready. Change the subject as gently and diplomatically as possible, and quietly withdraw.

Check the local papers and bookstores for lectures on the sixth sense, and invite a friend to join you. If you can't find anyone, go alone. Maybe your teammates are already there, waiting for you. Also, always pray for support, and then be open to receiving it. Happily, evolution is prevailing, and six-sensory people are

emerging in droves. These days it's becoming less and less difficult to connect with such kindred spirits if you really want to.

SIX-SENSORY WISDOM:

Go, team!

SECRET #18

One of the most common traits of six-sensory people is the ability to publicly acknowledge and express our vibes, no matter whom we interact with. Comfortably chatting about our intuitive sensations and experiences with others—starting with our psychic support team and then the world at large—without hesitation takes us a long way toward the goal of living a psychic life.

Five-sensory people rarely discuss their vibes because their ego says they're not real, or not real enough. This keeps their intuition under house arrest. But we six-sensory people love to talk about our intuitive experiences with abandon, and we have many colorful ways of doing so because it's such a colorful world. For example, whenever my friend Julia feels her sixth sense tap her on the shoulder, she says, "I'm getting marching orders," or "My guidance says . . . ," while Scott, a restaurateur and newly awakened intuitive, says, "I'm getting that feeling again." I say, "My vibes, or my spirit, tells me that . . ." because when I feel vibrations, I know that my spirit is talking to me.

Talking about your sixth sense freely and without embarrassment or apology opens the door for it to come into your life. Just like giving a baby a name when it's born, talking respectfully or even joyfully about your sixth sense gives it life. The key isn't so much how you express your intuitive inner world, but that you *do* express it, and with confidence and authority.

I want people to know about my sixth sense—not to shock or to seek approval, but because I love to share what makes my life work so well. Yet, as my client Jay told me, "I don't quite know how to tell others about my vibes because in my world, people don't talk about these things. I want to share how great my intuitive flashes are and how they help me, but I worry about what people will think.

"Still, my vibes are really exciting, and when I *do* talk about them, I get good results. People are fascinated, and even if they laugh, it's more because they aren't sure what to do or how to react—not because they dismiss what I'm saying. Some even wish they had vibes like I do."

Not only does talking about our intuitive world validate it for us, but we six-sensory folks like to talk openly because it's a powerful means of bridging our inner creative soul to our outer conscious world, inviting even more intuitive information to come through.

For example, I once told my sister about an intuitive dream I had about going to the ocean with a great group of people who were singing, healing, dancing, and having a wonderful time. As I talked to her, I got the strong feeling that it was a prophetic dream, and that I'd be doing what I dreamed about very soon even though I'm not a beach person. And my sister told me that *she'd* had a similar dream about doing a healing workshop in Hawaii. So our shared, combined dreams led to the creation of our most powerful joint workshop, "Translucent You," which we teach once a year in Hawaii. We sing, dance, play, do intuitive readings, give people healing massage therapy, and do art work and visioning as a way to completely heal the participants' psychic wounds and reclaim their intuitive voice. We have 13 healers and teachers on our staff, and together we create an awesome experience for all concerned. Had we not shared our dreams, and had I not felt that flood of psychic urgency when we spoke, we never would have devised this healing work, and we would have missed the joy it brings to everyone involved.

Talking about your vibes helps you process and examine what's contained in your inner treasure chest. Sharing your intuitive feelings helps pull them out, gives them life in the conscious world, and puts them to good use. Your sixth sense works in many ways—in symbols, pictures, key words, feelings, dreams, and metaphors. The intuitive realm has a language of its own, and in speaking about it, you can often translate and develop their meaning, thus providing your life with more riches as you do.

When I do intuitive readings for clients, I often feel as if I'm following a trail of clues. Thoughts, feelings, and images pop up as I go, and I never know what I'm going to say until I say it. I'm usually just as surprised to hear some of my insights as my clients are. And when I investigate my own problems, I speak aloud, even if I'm alone. Vocalizing invites my guides to jump in at any moment with solutions I'm unaware of—the more I talk about the problem, the more the solutions come. For instance, I was struggling over whether to take a trip to Menton, France, this summer because it would be expensive, inconvenient, and possibly conflict with my work commitments. Yet as I mulled it over with my husband, I heard myself saying, "I need to go. It'll be the last time I can visit the hotel where I lived 20 years ago when I was a student over there."

The hotel was a place I loved and held dear in my heart, so the possibility that it might soon be gone helped me make up my mind right away. Even though I had nothing to back up my vibes with, I made the reservation and resolved to let the other things in my life work around it. Ten days later I received a letter from my friend in Menton, saying that the hotel was being turned into condos, so this was the last year that it would be a hotel. I got tickets just in time to go, reconvene with my buddy, and revisit this sacred (to me) place before it was gone forever.

AN IMPORTANT ELEMENT in talking about your intuitive feelings is having the vocabulary to do so comfortably without bias, restraint, or self-consciousness. Now, I'm very comfortable with the word *psychic* when discussing my intuitive sense. I really love the word, but I'm definitely in the minority on this one. For many people, the word still has many superstitious or negative connotations, so they flinch when they hear it and don't feel comfortable using it to describe themselves.

Are you one of those people? Do you cringe when you see or hear the word *psychic?* If so, don't worry about it. It makes no difference what you call your sixth sense, as long as you call it *something,* and you can talk about it freely. Try using "my gut," "my instinct," "my radar," "my flash," or even "my wise and eternal wisdom." You can even call it "Bozo" for all it matters, just as long as you express your sixth sense positively so that you can continue to make room for it in your life. Just like a newborn baby, once it's here, you have to make a place for it—you can't stuff a baby back into the womb, and you can't stuff yourself back into the psychic closet. Once you talk about it, you won't want to stop.

Seasoned six-sensory people who follow their intuitive sense are enthusiastic and even proud of their insights. Their vibes make their lives easier, and they love to say so. People stuck halfway between the five- and six-sensory worlds have the urge to share and process their intuitive insights, but they tend to hesitate or be silent because they often don't know how to explain their victories.

Fence-sitters hedge, by saying, "I had a weird feeling," "Something bizarre happened," or "I have this odd sensation"—in other words, they couch their conversations in qualifiers that water their vibes down. I give them an A for effort; however, if *you* want to fully use your psychic sense, you'll have to do better than that. Your intuition is gold, so it should be gathered with appreciation and affection and shared enthusiastically rather than with qualifiers. Try saying, "I just had a terrific inspiration," "I just had an incredible feeling that . . . ," or "My inner genius tells me . . . ," and see what you get back from others and from your spirit. In my experience, the more I appreciate my psychic voice, the more it rewards me with even more genius information, so I get a double bonus.

I'm not suggesting that you exaggerate, because that too is an ego trap, and it will invite resistance. Just speak about your inner voice with respect and appreciation, which will show that you value it. (I've seen a few appreciative six-sensory people wake up some five-sensory folks to their intuition by simply describing their sixth sense with deep affection.) The more you pave the way from your inner creative laboratory to your outer conscious world through innovative words and easy expression, the better you build a bridge for your Higher Self to guide you day to day.

Six-Sensory Practice

This week, speak up and share your vibes, starting with your team members, and then with others. What words do you use to describe what you feel? Also, look for ways in which other people talk about their vibes, such as when your boss says, "I have a hunch that won't work," or when your spouse says, "I don't get a good feeling about that."

Talk about your intuitive feelings positively, such as "I have a great idea (or a helpful instinct)" instead of "This feels weird." If you think of your soul as offering you "pearls of wisdom" instead of "strange feelings," then you should express those pearls with grace, humor, and style. Be creative when describing your intuition by using expressions that acknowledge your psychic sense without attracting trouble. You might avoid the word *psychic* when talking about your intuition in your board meeting, for instance, but if you say "my hit," "my sense," or "my gut reaction," I can assure you that no one will even give it a second thought.

Decide what to say and to whom. Be inventive and make a list of 20 ways to describe your six-sensory world without hesitation, such as: *my vibes, my instinct, my gut, my feeling, a hunch, a sense, a hit, my guides, my radar, my angels* (which seems to get approval more often than any other expression).

It doesn't matter which words you use, as long as you talk about your intuitive thoughts and feelings in a positive, appreciative, and enthusiastic way. Share your victories with joy, and see how it elicits even more psychic gold.

SIX-SENSORY WISDOM:

Know that it's all in how you say it.

SECRET #19

FAKE IT TILL YOU MAKE IT

Several years ago, my husband, my daughters, and I went to an outdoor shopping mall to enjoy a warm summer evening. First we window-shopped, then we stopped for an ice-cream cone, and finally we strolled to a children's play area in the center of the mall to relax and watch the kids enjoy themselves.

As we sat down to eat our ice cream, we noticed a couple sitting across from us with their two-year-old. My older daughter, Sonia, impulsively stood (ice-cream cone still in hand), skipped around the parameter of the play area, kicked up her heels, and then plopped down next to me. Not to be outdone, her sister, Sabrina, leapt to her feet and did exactly what Sonia did, before coming to sit next to her sister.

The toddler, fascinated by my daughters' every move, watched them very closely. After the girls had sat down, the little boy turned to his father, who also had an ice-cream cone, and demanded that he hand it over, which he reluctantly did. With the cone in his hand and eyeballing the girls all the while, the little boy attempted to skip around the play area just as he'd seen them do, managing to mimic them to a tee . . . for about five feet, at which point, he lost his balance, tripped, and buried his left eye in the cone.

It was a hilarious and poignant moment that demonstrated once again how much we learn from imitating others. Our role models invite us into new experiences—unfortunately, when it comes to living a six-sensory life, not many of us have had positive role models to follow. More often than not, we've been told that six-sensory living is a gift, special to the selective and freaky few who either hang out in shady storefronts behind crystal balls or show up on late-night infomercials touting their dial-a-psychic hotlines. In either case, most evolving people are neither attracted nor compelled to replicate anything nearing these circuslike psychic offerings, and I don't blame them.

Infomercial psychics and storefront spiritual advisors are not true representatives of the six-sensory life, and like everything else five-sensory, they should be left in the Dark Ages. These fringe characters have no more psychic sense than anyone else, but they *do* have the ability to manipulate and prey upon the uneducated and superstitious. In fact, they don't want the rest of us to evolve at all because it would put them out of business.

What's important now, as you cross that final threshold into a creative, artful, six-sensory life, is to find inspiring role models who demonstrate, moment to moment, what living in spirit and operating from the heart really looks like—and then act like they do. Not having positive and compelling role models to show you six-sensory living can prevent you from enjoying an extraordinary life, while those who *do* represent the six-sensory life positively will become your greatest allies.

Many people are just scared beginners who want to step out of the closet of intuitive living, but they don't know how to do it gracefully and with style. Finding truly inspiring six-sensory people and walking in their footsteps will allow you to practice navigating your sixth sense in a gentle, subtle way that's nonthreatening and relaxed, not to mention tried and true.

Years ago, before author Julia Cameron was my friend (or even knew me), she began having consistent and unexplained psychic feelings, hunches, and inspirations. Uneasy, and not wanting to look like Madame Sophia at the corner psychic shop, she consulted a psychotherapist friend and confessed her anxiety at being so psychically aware: "I worry that I'll look like a freak, or people will think I'm a nut."

He listened to her for a while, and then quite ingeniously said, "The problem isn't your functioning sixth sense, Julia. The problem is that you have no positive role models to teach you how to use it and how to wear it publicly. Do you know anyone who is both six-sensory and graceful? Someone who is comfortable with their psychic sense and is as normal as you or I? Someone who can maybe even show you how to benefit from this gift so that it will serve you?"

His question opened her up to a new possibility, which led her to me. I showed her what I was taught: that being six-sensory can indeed be graceful, creative, and fun—there's nothing freaky or undignified about it. As I've said all along, being intuitive is a natural art that you can refine with practice.

After working with Julia, I reflected on my own six-sensory role models. There was my mom, who was beautiful, sophisticated, and brilliantly creative, and yet as grounded and practical about life as one can be. Then there were Dr. Tully and Charlie Goodman, two elegant, well-traveled, educated, and articulate men whose intuition was artful, high-minded, and oriented toward healing and spiritual growth. And my mentors, LuAnn Glatzmaier and Joan Smith, were exquisite, intelligent, and worldly women who were highly educated and wrote, counseled, taught, and created endless and beautiful works of art. Not one of these people were weird or "woo-woo," as so many people fear; in fact, each was a very ethical, responsible, and kind individual. They were all my inspirations, and their psychic expressions were like music to my soul. I used these people as my psychic and ethical baseline—I modeled their perspectives, replicated their views, and held to their standards until I developed my own sixth sense and integrity. I frolicked in their playground until it became my own . . . and then I became the one to invite the new kids on the block to play with me.

Finding your own six-sensory role models may be difficult because six-sensory people are often subtle, so you'll have to rely upon your ability to see them. Start by noting who's around you: Intuitives won't have neon signs flashing, but they do shine. The light will be their aura and self-confidence, the sparkle of their generous laugh and enthusiasm for life. Six-sensory folks don't usually attract attention to themselves intentionally, but others are often naturally drawn to them. Intuitives aren't always vocal about their vibes, but they don't hide it. Like having a sophisticated ear for music or a developed eye for beauty, six-sensory people have a talent for vibration, and they follow it.

Do you know any creative and courageous people who follow their heart, listen to their gut, trust their feelings, speak their truth, or act on their instincts without hesitation (or melodrama)? If so, you're in luck. Watch these individuals carefully, study them, and model yourself on them. Like a karaoke singer entering the stage for the first time, sing their song with the same enthusiasm they do, even if it feels strange. It will only feel this way in the beginning—with practice, it will become familiar until you make it your song. In other words, fake it till you make it. Eventually, you'll hear and write your own soul's music.

My student Chris wanted to be a singer from the time she was a young girl. Complete songs would rush into her head, mostly before she fell asleep at night. She knew she was channeling this music, but was shooed away from this explanation by her parents, who feared that being six-sensory was weird and abnormal. So Chris, not wanting such a stigma, distanced herself from her intuitive gifts and viewed them as unappealing. She laughed at those who were psychic or talked about channeling until she came to my workshop. That's where she met Jason, a very talented six-sensory composer who told her how *he* used channeling to compose several published symphonies.

Jason's love of music, along with the way he worked and his enthusiasm for his psychic inspiration, opened Chris's mind once again. And his warm, generous, healing spirit, which was so beautifully conveyed in his compositions, opened her heart as well. Jason became Chris's psychic role model. (Frankly, I was disappointed that she didn't choose me, but I think it was because he was cuter.) Modeling after Jason was exactly what Chris needed to reclaim her power. "I'm doing psychic karaoke, Sonia," she said. "I'm singing Jason's spirit, and I love it because it's exactly what I want to sing for myself. He gives me the courage and the style I needed."

So if *you* want to be a creative, confident, inwardly guided six-sensory being, study and model every creative intuitive you find. This is how we *human* beings learn—and how we *spiritual* beings find our true voice. But be selective when you choose your six-sensory role models: Pick those who inspire, create, and experience life joyfully with style, grace, and integrity; those exceptional people who enjoy their psychic abilities and share them in a loving and grounded way. The best way to identify good six-sensory role models is to perceive who among you are happy and love their life, sure signs that they're using all their senses well. Ask them what their secret is, and then use it.

Being intuitive is an art that can be mastered in the same way you master anything—by being a student and finding good teachers. Work alongside your peers, practicing your art as you apprentice with inspiring role models. Eventually, like a journeyman stepping out on his own, let life be the next teacher and your mistakes be the exams. Gracefully, over time, with patience, persistence, and practice, you'll come to master being you. That's what the higher way of six-sensory living leads to: becoming your fully enlightened, faithful self—not only the you that you want to be, but also the you that God designed you to be.

To get you started, I invite you to consider choosing me as your first six-sensory role model and sing psychic karaoke with me—soon, you will be singing your own six-sensory song.

Six-Sensory Practice

This week, open your eyes, ears, and heart, and search for your intuitive role models. Who is your psychic hero? Who sings your song and plays where you want to? What about these people can you imitate? Don't limit yourself—find as many sources of inspiration as possible. Walk their walk, talk their talk, dance their dance, sing their song—emulate them in every way. Is it what you want to do? Do you love it? If so, tell them. And keep singing until you're vocalizing your own creative, intuitive genius.

SIX-SENSORY WISDOM:

Stick with your people.

SECRET #20

LOOK BEHIND THE SCENES

Just as we telepathically communicate with one another on the physical plane, so do we connect with our angels and spirit guides on a higher plane. We have a very intimate link with our spirit helpers (guides who show us around the spiritual plane) at all times—all we have to do to receive their assistance is open our heart.

If you want guidance from angelic forces, you can access it by praying. In addition to asking for general assistance, you can also seek the support of specific angels for help on particular projects. If, for instance, you're a musician, or you want to undertake musical projects, you can pray to the angels of music to help you. If you're a writer, you can ask the angels of communication for aid. If you're looking for a new home or renovating your current residence, the "housing angels" can help you. The same goes for angels of travel, of healing, for the protection of the family and of children, and for any other particular concern. There are angels for every need, and they're happy to be called upon to assist you.

I personally pray for help from my teaching, parenting, and relationship angels, to name a few. And I'm still grateful to my cooking angel for getting me out of hot water a few summers ago. As I said earlier, my husband is a very good cook and takes a great deal of time and care to prepare meals, especially for guests. Well, on this particular day, Patrick had invited some good friends over for dinner. He spent all day preparing a pork roast for barbecuing, then he placed it on the grill and told me to watch it for a few minutes while he went to pick up our daughter, Sonia.

I sat next to the barbecue for about five minutes when the phone rang. It was my oldest and dearest friend, whom I hadn't spoken to in more than six years. Needless to say, I forgot about the roast until I heard a terrible scream from the backyard. It was Patrick, who was yelling, "Oh, my Gawd! The barbecue is on fire!" I immediately hung up the phone and ran out to see what was happening, only to discover my husband holding a large fork, on which the roast was speared—in flames. (Apparently the grease from the roast had collected and had set the meat on fire.)

Just as Patrick doused the flames, our guests arrived. Furious that I hadn't watched the roast after he had worked so hard to prepare it, and feeling embarrassed that we now had nothing to serve, Patrick silently glared at me and went to answer the door. Desperately, I begged my angels for help.

Patrick stormed back with the guests and announced, "I might as well tell you that Sonia didn't watch the roast, so it caught on fire. We now have nothing to eat."

"Wait," I said, praying like mad. "We're not sure the meat is ruined."

"Why bother?" Patrick sneered, but I insisted that he cut into the roast anyway. To everyone's amazement, the meat was seared to absolute perfection. It was the most delicious roast we've ever had—even Charlie Trotter, the most famous chef in Chicago, couldn't have done a better job. The dinner was a smashing success, and I thanked my cooking angels over and over again for saving the day.

I believe that every undertaking will unfold much easier and with more peace and sweetness if you just ask your angels to assist you. After all, they're present and ready to assist in every situation. I've never known an angel to let someone down in all my years of working with them. But your spirit team doesn't have to be limited to angels—saints, prophets, and deities are also available to help. If you've been raised Catholic, you're surely familiar with the various saints and their ability to assist us from the Other Side. My personal favorites are St. Joseph, the patron saint of houses; St. Anthony of Padua, the patron saint of finding things; St. Thérèse, "The Little Flower," the patron saint of love; St. Christopher, the patron saint of travel; St. Jude, the patron saint of hopeless causes; and, of course, my most beloved favorite—Mother Mary, the feminine face of God, who brings compassion and tenderness to all.

It doesn't matter if you seek support from a deity who resides outside of your spiritual tradition, for the higher powers don't make any distinctions. For example, my American friend Annette routinely prays to the Indian goddess Kali, while my Christian friend Steven prays to Buddha for support. My Jewish friend Dan asks St. Anthony to help him find new accounts, and he's been amazed at the help he's received. One of my Catholic friends asks the great White Eagle in the Native American tradition to assist, and I regularly ask Gaia, Greek mythology's Divine Mother, to help me out.

To ask any spiritual force for aid, simply focus your heart on where you need assistance or are in pain, and then say "Help." The Universe will give you access to all aspects of itself, so if you focus on receiving help in a certain area, you'll telepathically send that communication forward, attracting a resonating response in return. So if you invoke the spiritual help of deities, these benevolent higher forces will respond.

Some people worry that asking angels, saints, or gods and goddesses for help is worshiping false gods. Don't worry—that's your ego talking again. There's *nothing* wrong with this practice; in fact, you're accessing God in all of His/Her forms and faces, and in all ways. But if you don't feel comfortable reaching out to and communicating with these many forms of loving assistance, you don't have to. You can simply ask God to put His/Her helpers on the job without your knowing who's been assigned to it.

You may also be offered assistance by those you've known or even heard about who have crossed over into Spirit. People do this naturally, and many cultures make it part of their daily spiritual practice, invoking the wisdom and assistance of their ancestors to help them. Their spirit lives on and can still connect to us, so it makes sense that they're there to help us. You can also telepathically ask for help from those on the Other Side who, while they were alive, achieved great success in a certain area, such as art, music, medicine, and even government. For example, I have two very dear friends who routinely ask for guidance with respect to their musical compositions from past composers such as Richard Rodgers. And I once knew a budding young artist who constantly struggled with painting techniques until he psychically sought the assistance of Michelangelo and Raphael to help him get the hang of it. I'm not sure they ever answered him, but I do know that he quit complaining and started to enjoy himself.

I have regular dreams in which I'm being taught by three of my most important spirit guides—13th-century French Catholic bishops named De Leon, Lucerne, and Maurice—who instruct me on the secret doctrines of the church and on the deeper meaning of the tarot. These nocturnal classes have helped me channel some of the most meaningful information I've ever received and are perhaps the greatest source of intuitive guidance in my work as a spiritual teacher.

Keep in mind that when you ask for guidance, you should always use common sense. Would you have trusted a certain individual's input before they passed? If not, don't trust it now. Some psychic forces are just energetic vagabonds, lost souls who are eager to stow away or hitch a ride with you if you let them. You see, we don't automatically evolve into spiritual consciousness the minute we die—whether in body or not, we still have to grow, and we pick up after death where we left off in life. For instance, my student Emily's husband drank and gambled himself into an early grave at the age of 59. Shortly after he died, Emily came to my class to help her heal from the loss. Within weeks she began to feel his spirit communicating with her, which comforted her greatly because, in spite of his failings, she missed him terribly. Soon after, she began having dreams in which he advised her to gamble. Believing that he was trying to make up for his earthly mistakes, Emily trusted the dreams and did as he suggested.

Within three months she lost over $3,000.

Feeling distraught and confused, Emily came to see me. "How can this be happening to me again?" she cried. "He told me how much to bet on certain horses, and each time I lost. What's going wrong?"

"Nothing," I said. "But he's just as addicted to gambling without a body as he was when he had one—and now he's using you. Stop giving him credit where none is due, and quit gambling at once."

Those who have passed out of body unexpectedly often hang around for a while, especially if they were insensitive about their soul or about moving into the light. And because they're displaced with nothing better to do, they'll gladly offer their two cents' worth if you're willing to listen. This is especially true of souls who were largely ignored in their earthly form. If you pay attention to them now, they're delighted—yet their input is almost always useless and can even be damaging. So if you ever feel that a soul is connecting to you but not contributing, simply command them into the light and ask their angels to come and get them because they've lost their way.

Many beginning six-sensory students who don't take the necessary steps to get grounded and be discerning end up with low-level spirits holding their attention and taking them hostage to their endless and nonsensical ramblings. For example, I once had a neighbor who was contacted by a spirit guide who told her that she was an enlightened being. No offense, but this should have been her first clue that she was connecting to a spirit with questionable credentials. A good intuitive guide never flatters and doesn't tell you you're special—after all, on a soul level we're all the same, but at different levels of awakening. My neighbor believed this nonsense and started to act as though she deserved special attention, even expecting others to pay homage to her. Of course, there were no takers in her scheme, and her family and friends dropped her like a hot potato.

Confused about why no one would listen to her vibes, she came to me for advice. I told her that you can always tell if vibes are reliable by the results they bear: If they're from a higher plane, they'll bring about improvement and closeness to others. Because she believed the flattery of her displaced spirit, she was rejected and resented by those close to her, and everyone considered her a nut. I washed her windshield of self-delusion, assuring her that although she was important and lovable, there was nothing particularly special about her. And my guides suggested that rather than pose as an enlightened being, she'd be better off doing some enlightened service, such as working in a soup kitchen, where the light she did have could shine upon others. Accepting my counsel, she turned in her turban, put on an apron, and began helping out at the local church's homeless lunch program.

WE'RE ALL EQUAL SPIRITUAL BEINGS, interconnected and in various stages of unfolding consciousness. At our deepest level, we're one body and spirit—therefore, any suggestion to the contrary isn't worth the time of day, so ignore it. Out-of-body beings can appeal to the ego, and if they haven't made the transition from ego law to spiritual law, they'll keep trying to get to you, even on the Other Side. So it's very important to be discerning when receiving guidance—you don't want to be distracted by what I call "psychic riffraff," or drivel that flatters and offers no substantial assistance. True guidance is balanced, sensible, and never tells you what to do. It simply offers supportive suggestions and leaves the decision up to you, respecting your freedom to make your own choices and mistakes. If the message you're receiving is frightening, leaves you feeling uncomfortable, or suggests that its way is the only way, telepathically change the channel immediately because it's definitely not from a Higher Source—and it's a waste of your time. Simply say, "I send you into the light. Be gone." And then let go. (You can also ask for help from Spirit to keep you protected from the guidance of lost souls.)

As a soul-based, six-sensory person, you have access to support from the entire hierarchy of universal light beings, beginning with people who have crossed over, to your Creator Him/Herself. Use this ability to connect to Divine Wisdom to your advantage. When you feel weak or confused, ask for help, inspiration, protection, and direction, then listen to what comes through. Spirit is subtle, so pay close attention. When guidance does come through, see how it leaves you feeling: If it's from the Light, it will leave you feeling that very way—light and energized.

Six-Sensory Practice

This week, become aware of assistance you're getting from Spirit. Realize that you have an entire psychic support system available to help you at all times. If you feel vulnerable, ask your angels for protection. If you're working on a particular project, ask the angels in that area to assist you. If you have any desire to tune in to psychic mentors from another age, invite them to help you. If you're missing someone who has crossed over to the Other Side, send him or her love, and if you want, ask for his or her support. But be certain to ask only for loving, useful help grounded in light and love from these benevolent forces. Carefully discern the quality of guidance that you receive, and always thank your Divine Helpers for their loving assistance.

SIX-SENSORY WISDOM:

Call in the troops.

SECRET #21

GO BACK TO SCHOOL

I learned early on that as we grow spiritually, our vibes become more accurate, our guides' ability to assist greatly opens up, and we find that we actually have many different kinds of guides who do different things for us. I've had as many as 33 guides working with me at one time, especially when I'm teaching a psychic class. Sure, I show up as the teacher, but my spirit guides do the instructing.

We all have a particularly important group of guides in addition to those I've already mentioned in this book: our *spirit teachers,* whose primary purpose is to help us evolve spiritually. They oversee our personal soul lessons, or the unique soul curriculum that each of us has selected before we incarnated into this lifetime. These lessons reflect our individual soul ambitions and help us focus on our weaknesses so that we can move past them and love more easily. In other words, this is the primary soul purpose of our lives.

The focus of my six-sensory practice has been to help people recognize and understand their soul curriculum. I tune in to clients' past life histories and look at their souls' evolution from lifetime to lifetime, in the same way you might look at a student's progress from kindergarten to college. I can see what lesson my clients are assigned and what they need to learn. I can also see their blind spots and the soul assignments they keep

143

flunking, which cause them to suffer. I see all this with the help of my teacher guides and those of my clients—together they psychically show me what the clients are here for and what they must focus on to grow and find peace of mind and a fulfilled sense of purpose. My teacher guides are very busy and keep me in training because *my* soul curriculum is to help raise the awareness of others to Divine Guidance. This is why I use my intuitive abilities as a model when I teach.

It's important to get in touch with your teacher guides, for they'll influence you to become self-reflective and honest about your life and improve those areas that cause you difficulty. They'll also relay strong messages to get you to grow spiritually—spirit teachers have been known to bring books to your attention or have you turn on radio and television programs that address your particular areas of weakness. They'll also connect you to people who can instruct you on the earthly plane if you're open to learning. As a spiritual teacher, it never fails to surprise me when I see how resistant people are to learning new things. They don't want to know that their troubles may be the result of poor choices and, therefore, could be alleviated or solved by learning; instead, they'd rather blame someone else—even evil spirits from the dark side. Yet the entire point of incarnating into a physical body is to evolve in a continuous classroom. The only way to finish the curriculum is to die, and even then you'll just begin a new one. But right now, you're here in this life to learn as much as possible.

It's important to know that teacher guides work in very subtle but direct ways. They usually come in those moments when you feel you're hitting rock bottom, and they get your attention by arranging exposure to relevant information—such as brochures, announcements, or invitations by strangers to lectures and workshops; or they suggest that you turn on the radio or TV when a guest you should hear is being interviewed. A favorite maneuver of spirit teachers is to have a book fall off a shelf in a store or library and hit you on the head. For example, my client Catherine wanted to learn more about her psychic sense for years, but never did. "One day I went to Barnes & Noble," she told me, "because

I had an overwhelming urge to read something new. I didn't know what I was looking for, so I was poking around the meta-physical section when suddenly a copy of *The Psychic Pathway* fell off the top shelf and hit me on my head.

"I was so surprised that I started laughing! Reading your book led me to your workshop, which led me to the study of energy medicine. Now I'm apprenticing to be a Reiki healer and an intu-itive channel—not only am I discovering that I have a gift for healing, but I've never been happier and more fulfilled in my life. When people ask me how I got into my field, I say it literally hit me over the head."

Another way in which a teacher guide works is through mes-sengers, people who suddenly step forward and make recom-mendations for learning for no apparent reason, even though it may be uncomfortable for them to do so. For instance, a teacher guide must have enlisted the help of the person standing next to my husband in a grocery store line because she unexpectedly told him, "You must be a painter or a poet."

He laughed and replied, "No, I just want to be."

"Do you paint?"

"Yes, but not well and not often."

"Do you write poetry?"

"Sometimes, but I'm only an amateur."

"Then you *are* a painter and a poet," she remarked. "You just don't practice enough."

When my husband told me about that conversation, I said that his spirit teacher was talking through that lady: "She prob-ably didn't know what came over her to say those things, but I've been saying them for years. I guess your teacher guides thought a stranger might have more impact."

He got the message and started painting again the next day—and was clearly happier for it.

My client Alice's spirit teachers took a similar approach with her. Struggling financially for as long as she could remember, Alice lived in a state of constant drama. She never thought about examining her life or imagining that it could be different; instead, she just lived from crisis to crisis. I told her that she needed to learn about money because in most of her past lives she was a servant or slave who never had any. One of her soul assignments was to make money instead of expecting others to support her. I suggested that she get teachers to help her learn financial responsibility, but she wasn't interested—she thought that marrying a rich man was the solution. I told her I didn't want to burst her bubble, but I psychically saw that this wasn't an option for her.

"So that's why I never date?" she asked, as a lightbulb went off in her head.

"Yes," I replied. "You've blocked that possibility in this lifetime so that you could grow. I'm sorry, but there's no sugar daddy in the picture for you."

Even though it may feel like a bitter pill at the moment, people are always relieved on some level when they hear the truth and what they must do to move forward. Alice left without asking me for advice on how to learn about money, so I didn't offer. (I learned long ago that, as an intuitive, I should never work harder for someone's clarity than they're willing to work for themselves.)

I trusted that Alice's spirit teachers would take it from there, and they did. You can imagine her surprise when the next day at lunch, as she was reciting her daily laundry list of financial complaints and struggles, a co-worker she barely knew blurted out, "Have you ever heard of Debtors Anonymous?"

Taken aback, and remembering what I'd told her the day before, she said, "No, I haven't. What is it?"

"I'm not really sure," the person replied, "but I think it's a free program for teaching people like you how to handle money better."

Alice felt a little weirded out until she realized that her spirit teachers were on the scene giving her an opportunity to grow. So she inquired, "How do I find out where to contact them?"

"I don't know," her co-worker answered. "Try calling Information."

As Alice drove home that evening, she heard an interview on public radio featuring a famous actor who was recounting his life, particularly his gambling problem and how he'd solved it. Alice hated to admit it, but she too had gambled quite a bit, so she listened intently as the actor explained how he'd cleaned up his act by, among other things, joining Debtors Anonymous. Including my reading, Alice had received the same message three times in a 24-hour period. Obviously, someone was trying to tell her something.

"Okay, I surrender," Alice said aloud. "I admit it. I need help." A deep feeling of peace quickly enveloped her, replacing the constant anxiety of the previous three years. The minute she got home she called Information and found a Debtors Anonymous group in her area. "It was a turning point," she later told me. "It was the first time I ever received a real education in financial responsibility. With the group's help, I stopped my crazy spending habits—and it didn't cost a penny! I'm so grateful that my guides gave me the kick in the pants I needed to get financially sober. I was desperately in denial and didn't even know it."

Even intuitives must grow in this lifetime—we're not exempt from learning. Anyone who thinks that being six-sensory excuses them from self-examination and growth should be avoided. Being six-sensory means being a sensitive channel to Spirit, not being a know-it-all. We're all at different levels of evolution, and the more ambitious we are, the steeper the learning curve. I make it a practice to always learn new things from those who are stronger, brighter, and more accomplished in certain areas than I am. However, many years ago I did feel that because I was six-sensory I should know all sorts of things without being taught. This put an enormous—and unnecessary—strain on me. When I began to listen to my teacher guides, I discovered that they wanted me to be a perpetual student who would probably never reach the top of her learning curve. I was relieved to know that being a pupil, even an advanced one, was important to my psychic sense, not an indication of failure. The more I learned about myself and how I tick, the better my intuitive readings for others became.

Several years ago, feeling particularly bogged down by too many responsibilities and not enough balance, I asked my teacher guides for help. In response, I was guided to visit a counselor friend. "I know there must be something I need to learn in order to feel better, I just don't know what it is," I admitted to her. "Do you have any ideas?"

"I just heard about a workshop called 'The Hoffman Process,'" she said, handing me some literature. "It might be what you need—why don't you check it out?"

Just holding the brochure in my hand felt right, and I knew that I had to go. Acting on pure instinct and guidance, I cleared my schedule for the next ten days (which was no small feat), and was on my way 48 hours later. This proved to be one of the most profound healing classes I'd ever attended. It helped me clear the debris of self-sabotaging patterns I'd been stuck in for years and opened me up to even more profound intuitive channeling and healing. The way the workshop fell into my lap, timing and all, was a lifesaver. I knew that my teacher guides had led me to this instruction as part of my spiritual growth.

I'M OFTEN AMUSED, but at times frustrated, by the fact that people resist taking advice from their teacher guides, especially when it would clearly help them. For example, Alex, a client who was a very gifted performer, made no effort to support that part of his life. Instead, he settled for being a financial consultant, selling services he didn't believe in. It was no wonder this guy was unfulfilled and restless—it didn't take an intuitive like me to figure that one out. I tried countless times to relay a message to him from his teacher guides that he should take some creative risks and join an improvisational theater class, but he tuned me out each time. "I'm not an actor," he'd say, even though my sixth sense said he was, but he was afraid. We had the same conversation over and over for three years with no change.

One day Alex showed up with several catalogs from the Chicago Center for the Performing Arts. Smiling, he shook the literature at me and asked, "Are you responsible for sending me these?"

Looking them over, I said, "No, but I wish I were, because it's exactly where you need to go."

"I started receiving copy after copy of the same catalog every day for the past two weeks," he said. "I felt like the school was stalking me. Do you think someone's trying to tell me something?"

"Gee, I don't know, Alex. Given the past five intuitive readings you've had with me, what do you think?"

Alex took the hint and signed up for a basic improvisational class that day. The last I heard was that he loved acting and was still pursuing it. I don't know if he ever got any professional work, but that wasn't the point—what he got from the class was the opportunity to express his true self.

Teacher guides are inspiring, but to benefit from their messages, you have to take an honest look at how much you could still stand to learn. You must agree to be a student again: A willingness to do so throughout your entire life is basic to a true six-sensory life, for it opens up the avenues for your spirit teachers to lead you to fantastic opportunities and new facets of yourself every day.

It's interesting that in almost every reading I do, a teacher guide will show up, offering recommendations for learning that would greatly benefit the client's soul. Yet despite these suggestions, many people tune this guidance out and refuse to grow. They use excuses such as, "I'll just read a book," "I don't like groups," or "I don't have the time," even though being a student would bring new tools and forward movement and open them up to more ways to enjoy life.

I know that all the most meaningful leaps forward in creative expression and peace of mind in my life came with the help and loving assistance of both spirit and earthly teachers. For example, my teachers Dr. Tully and Charlie Goodman both emphasized in many ways that I should never assume I know anyone or anything completely, including myself, and to always be open to learning something new. It's been good advice. And my mentor LuAnn Glatzmaier continually reminds me that the greatest reason for being on this planet is to learn all that we possibly can about ourselves. I've made it an important part of my own spiritual practice to be a student in a new classroom at least twice a year, and to surround myself with teachers, mentors, and sources of inspiration.

I love being a student and always will be. In fact, one of my favorite sayings, which I often cite to students and clients who resist being open to learning, is taken from the *I Ching,* or *Book of Changes,* which states: "There is something very limited about an exclusively self-taught man."

Is refusing to learn from others limiting you? Is your ego easily threatened and blocking your spirit by thinking you know it all? The simple willingness to learn sets the stage for six-sensory opening. And the more you open your heart and mind to your spirit teachers, the more you'll be led to our earthly classrooms. The more help you have in becoming your authentic self, the more peaceful, loving, and joyful your life will be. Your spirit and earthly teachers are here to help you discover your authentic self and enjoy being who you really are.

With a beginner's mind and heart, the student mode keeps us receptive to the assistance available from all directions in heaven and on Earth. So keep your ego out of the way, and become a student again. See this as an opportunity to make life easier, not as a remedial effort. Practice saying, "I don't know, but I'm willing to learn." Then let your spirit teachers lead you to where you can do just that.

Six-Sensory Practice

Practice being more aware of your teacher spirit guides this week. They're not very far away—in fact, they're some of the first guides who will come though and get your attention. And to grease the wheels of learning, why not attend at least one new class in your community. Choose anything you've been meaning to study but have resisted or been unable to. It's okay to start small, such as signing up for a one-day seminar or weekend workshop instead of a full semester or one-year program. If you don't know where to begin, call community colleges, spiritual centers, and adult-education extension classes to ask for catalogs or syllabi.

Also, ask yourself if your spirit teachers have been trying to make contact with you. Have any books fallen on your head lately? Has anyone invited you to a lecture or a class or made you aware of a group that focuses on a specific area of learning that interests you? If so, do you recognize how your spirit teachers are using these people as messengers? They are, you know. If you want to be six-sensory, you need to recognize that one of an intuitive's primary orientations is how we're contacted by Spirit in order to grow, which is the most important assignment of our life.

As a way of discerning whether you really want to become six-sensory, ask yourself if you're accepting the spirit-guided assistance already coming through. Are you moved to seek new teachers? Are you open to reading interesting books or attending lectures? Are you willing to follow these spirit promptings from the Other Side and avail yourself of something fresh?

Six-sensory people are very honest, so it's now time to be honest about yourself. Can you easily recognize your limitations and be a student without feeling small or inferior? If so, you're on your way to six-sensory expansion. Don't make this too complicated—start by studying something fun. And be certain to see attaining knowledge as a way to make life easier, not as reform school. Learning isn't intended to fix you because you're broken, it only serves to empower you . . . and that's the whole point of becoming more intuitive in the first place.

SIX-SENSORY WISDOM:

Keep learning.

PART VI

The Six-Sensory Advantage

SECRET #22

EXPECT THE BEST

Perhaps one of the greatest distinctions between five-sensory and six-sensory people is that five-sensories worry about how they're going to make it in the world, whereas six-sensories always know that the Universe will be there to help them in every way. In other words, five-sensory people follow an ego-based set of rules, while six-sensory individuals follow spiritual law.

I believe that the greatest advantage in being six-sensory is feeling relieved of the need to figure life out. Trying to control the world is an all-consuming and exhaustive effort, and quite frankly, it's a useless pursuit. Those who do so pull back from life and never live in the way they want to. Fear of making a mistake or losing control—or any number of other imagined failures of the ego—keep more five-sensory people from living the lives they really want than anything else.

Take my client Yvonne, for instance. Yvonne was miserable being a travel agent and longed to work with animals, yet she couldn't figure out how to secure a job in this field. Fear of going broke, not finding a good job, and losing her insurance, among other things, kept her from pursuing her dream. She ignored her strong intuition and didn't do anything to even explore the possibilities. My encouragement didn't make a dent in her vigorous five-sensory belief that she wouldn't make it in a field she loved—her ego simply wouldn't let her consider quitting her job or doing something part-time.

Now contrast this with my client Karen, who was also unhappy in her job and who also felt drawn to work with animals. Unlike Yvonne, Karen was willing to trust her sixth sense and follow her feelings even if she wasn't sure where they'd lead. She told me, "I know it's right, even if I don't have a job. Do you think that if I trust my vibes and go on faith alone, I'll be okay?"

I had no doubt—I knew that Karen would prosper because spiritual law dictates this. I was her most enthusiastic cheerleader and suggested that the sooner she followed her vibes, the better. She soon began dog sitting and dog walking for a few friends. Then, one afternoon, her guides spoke in her ear, telling her, "Doggie day care." The name and idea struck her as amusing and smart, and at that moment she decided to expand her services and start a day-care service for dogs. She advertised in the local pet stores and newspapers, offering dog owners a place where she'd walk, feed, and play with their pooches for the day.

Within a month, Karen had ten rich (and some famous) clients clamoring for their dogs to get in to her doggie day care. She was running a full-time business before she'd even printed up her business cards, and she's been prospering and having fun with the dogs ever since. Unlike her five-sensory soul sister, Yvonne, Karen expected support from the Universe, and she got it. Now she's riding the energy waves of life, doing exactly what she wanted and loving every minute of it. Karen got rich and happy for trusting her spirit and following her psychic genius; Yvonne, on the other hand, got laid off. When last I spoke with her, I suggested that she call Karen (who knows—maybe she'd need some help with her business).

Most five-sensory people say no to their heart and spirit, while their six-sensory counterparts always say yes to their inner genius. To cross the bridge into six-sensory wonderland, stop listening to your ego and start to expect the best of the Universe to help you every day. Like soaring through the air on a trapeze, you must let go of five-sensory rules and grab on to Spirit. There will be a brief moment when you'll be cut free from the known, but guess what? In that moment, you'll be flying. It's only when you *don't* let go that you'll crash to the ground or dangle in midair doing nothing.

Knowing that the Universe will help you puts you in a vibratory state of receptivity, which creates a vacuum. Whenever a vacuum is created, spiritual law dictates that the Universe will rush in to fill it with its vibratory equivalent. In other words, you get what you expect. So if two people drive to downtown Chicago on a summer weekend night and one expects to find a parking space and the other doesn't, they'll both be right: The person who expects support will get it, while the one who doesn't, won't.

Expecting support from the Universe instantly raises your vibration to a six-sensory level because you remember the truth of who you are: an invaluable and precious child of God, not some lost and random nobody adrift at sea. In this way, you'll take your place in the garden of life and open up to receiving the blessings and support available to you. Even though some people are cynical and doubt this (ego ploy), I suggest that they try before they decide. Expectation is an energy magnet that draws to you whatever you ask for. Because I've always expected the best, I attract it again and again. Some call this luck; it's actually Divine Law.

Five-sensory people obsess endlessly over the "hows" of life: How will I make it? How will I meet someone who loves me? How can I sustain the romance I have now? How can I be sure of anything and everything? But six-sensory people don't concern themselves with *how*—they focus on what they want and what they can do to get it. They leave the hows of the Universe up to Divine Mystery.

In my 25 years of teaching people the way to manifest their dreams (and 35 years of doing it myself), I've never heard a single success story from a person who needed to know *how* before following a dream. My mother used to say, "If God gives you the idea, He'll give the way as well." I know from experience that this is absolutely true—the Universe has always been more creative about making my dreams come true than I could have ever been. I now know that all of life is really a creative dance with Spirit, and that we can't dance the part that isn't ours. We can't dictate the magic of life—we can only do our part to bring it about, and when we do, the magic of the Universe will rush in to meet us halfway.

One common illusion five-sensory folks have about six-sensory people is that we know everything in advance. The truth is that we rarely do, but we don't need to. We know what isn't working now, and we feel and trust that if we follow our inner wisdom, the Universe will take care of us like it does all its beautiful creations. The only thing we intuitives can guarantee is that ignoring our spirit and clinging to our intellect and fears will steal our joy and waste our life. We also know that if we're willing to do our part in following our heart, the Universe will show us the way to success, moment by magical moment.

Six-Sensory Practice

This week, expect the best from the Universe. Allow your mind and heart to open, and ask yourself how many wonderful gifts you can stand. Raise the mental and emotional ceiling of good things you allow yourself, and invite more support each hour of the day. When you go to work, expect the commute to be painless; expect to get the best parking space or seat on the train or bus; expect your boss, co-workers, and clients to appreciate you; expect people to smile at you and greet you; expect your meetings to go smoothly and your work to be brilliant. If you're single and looking for love, expect to meet someone who's fabulous and interested in you. If you're in a relationship, expect your partner to dazzle you with romance. When the phone rings, expect good news. When the mail comes, expect wonderful surprises, even presents. When confronted with a problem, expect easy and fast solutions. Above all, expect love and assistance to rain upon you all of your days.

SIX-SENSORY WISDOM:

Expect miracles.

SECRET #23

LOVE THE ADVENTURE

Five-sensory people often go through life with their foot on the brake (that is, they're hesitating, cautious, and fearful), while six-sensory people have their foot on the gas (they're open, enthusiastic, and adventurous). Five-sensory people following ego rules look for what's wrong and plan for trouble; six-sensory people expect the best from life, plan positively, and are open to life's gifts and opportunities. But most of all, five-sensory people tend to fear life—and six-sensory, intuitive people simply cannot get enough of it.

Being passionate about life tends to change your vibration from one of resistance and defense to one of attraction and receptivity. When you love life, life loves you back—so when you dive into it with exuberance and joy, life will reach out and enthusiastically embrace you. The more you love life by fully engaging in what feeds your soul, the more you spread that love around, and in doing so you heal yourself and others.

Life lovers have incredible charisma and charm, drawing people to them because their vibration is so soothing and positive. But being such a person isn't easy, nor is it an accident. It's much easier to be cynical and dark and argue for why life is miserable. The ego loves to suffer—and the louder, the better. Lovers of life say no to this death sentence, making intentional choices to appreciate and enjoy the gifts that life offers. They light up a room like the Christmas tree in New York City's Rockefeller Center. The Dalai Lama is such a lover, but so are many other folks in the world. For example, there's Ray, who works at my gym. His vibration is delightful—every other sound out of his mouth is a laugh. He's always inspiring others, telling jokes, offering suggestions, and letting people know how much he loves his life. Some days when I'm feeling drained and uninspired and don't feel like going to the gym, I go anyway just to get a dose of Ray. I once told him that life named him well, because he truly is a ray of sunshine.

I have another friend named Wendy who always looks for the best in any situation, appreciates the small stuff in life, and has an open heart and door for everyone. Being with her is like taking a mini-vacation—in her presence, I laugh a lot and find a lot to enjoy. We talk about what we love, from croissants in a Parisian café; to ice skating on the outdoor rink downtown at night; to Italian comedies, Indian food, and bargains at resale shops. Just talking to her is food for my soul.

To become a lover of being alive, dip your cup into the river of life and sip its nectar joyfully, rather than turning your back on it. Most five-sensory people refuse to taste life's sweetness until, as one highly deprived client said, "I can get all my ducks in a row." (Unfortunately, chasing and training "her ducks" to fall in line had wasted 50 years of her life—not one minute of which she had enjoyed.) You must recognize what feeds your spirit, and then give it to yourself without delay—*don't wait until all your problems are solved*. Nurture yourself by realizing what lifts your heart, tickles your funny bone, engages your curiosity, and stimulates your sense of wonder. Step up to life instead of running away from it—don't postpone your fun because you have serious matters to pursue first. As a true life lover once told me, "The minute a crisis hits, I go dancing. I'll deal with it better after I've danced."

DO YOU KNOW WHAT FEEDS YOUR SOUL and makes you a lover of life? Are you in touch with what brings you happiness and joy, making you content and spiritually fed? What affirms to you that life is good and worth living? You'll never discover what it is if you wait until the rushing river of life calms down long enough for you to reflect. You've got to step into the rapids, the rough-and-tumble roar of life, in order to find your soul's desires and delights. Take your moments *now*, not when you finish your responsibilities.

Here's an example of what I'm talking about from my own life. This past November was unusually warm for Chicago. The vibrant leaves on the trees splattered the skies with brilliant oranges, reds, and yellows, and the smell of fall was delicious. Because the weather was so gorgeous, Patrick and I decided to take an hour every afternoon and either go for a long bike ride or stroll along the lakefront near our home. Although it was difficult to attend to our normal demands and responsibilities, the satisfaction we derived from our afternoon excursions was so great that it was worth all the disruption. Not only did our daily dance with the beauty of the season fill our bodies with joy and contentment, it also created a vibration between us that made us feel as though we were young lovers again. As if that weren't enough of a gift, another magical thing occurred in our offices: Patrick and I both received numerous business calls from people inviting us to participate in new adventures. It was as though the more fun we had, the more the world wanted to play with us. While we were out nurturing our souls, life was nurturing us. That's the way the Universe works, and it's the best-kept secret of all.

Although letting go a little might frighten your ego, the more you enjoy yourself, the more you'll raise your vibration and attract good things. I especially recommend that those of you who feel abandoned and unloved pursue life with gusto. If you're lonely, stop turning your back on the playground of life and join in—start playing, and don't assume that no one wants to play with you. No matter what you think you want, love is all you're really seeking, so rather than wait for it to find you, reach out and grasp it right now.

One of the most striking observations I've made over my lifetime as an intuitive and healer is that countless people suffer from a sort of psychic anorexia—that is, they starve their souls of the sweet, nurturing elements of life and don't even think about what nurtures their spirits. Six-sensory, spiritual people know that feeding their soul is as important and necessary to their well-being as feeding their body is. Soul-starvation makes people bitter, angry, and resentful, creating a toxic vibration that causes others to recoil, leaving them isolated and lonely.

Most of us starve our souls without even realizing it: We do it when we gulp down unloved food; when we race through our days focused on the future, thus missing the scent of the flowers and the warmth of the sunshine; when we forget to go for a walk, look at the stars, enjoy a great conversation with a friend, or sit by the fire with a good book; when we watch too many newscasts or listen to too many tales of darkness, foregoing our bike rides, bubble baths, and playing with the dog; and when we give up romance, pleasure, and the enjoyment of small things. Instead, we should be drinking in and savoring these wonderful moments.

Julia Cameron understands how essential it is to the intuitive and creative spirit to feed the soul by advocating what she calls an *artist date,* or a once-a-week appointment to indulge in something for your soul to feast on. It can be anything from scouring secondhand stores to roller skating in the park, renting a foreign film and making a big bowl of popcorn, or gallery or museum hopping. Like a well that runs dry, the soul get used up quickly and needs to be replenished regularly. Doing so sprinkles what my friend Annette calls "fairy dust" in your life. It makes the ordinary sparkle, and attracts miracles and magic to your front door.

Are you willing to frolic in life's garden? Are you willing to feed and nurture your spirit? Are you able to stop your psychic anorexia and nourish your soul every day? Are you willing to sip the sweetness of life and then pass the cup of goodness to others? If you are, you'll experience all you desire and more. Nurturing your soul first and freely—or choosing to pursue what makes you happy so that you can infuse others with your enthusiasm—is basic to living in a six-sensory way.

If you feel stuck, change the channel and focus on what feeds your soul, and then do it. Recognize the feast of life placed before you—a good CD, a fresh cup of coffee, birds singing, a warm breeze, a walk through the neighborhood, a great novel. Only *you* know what nurtures your spirit, and when you find it, you'll bring light to yourself and those around you. The *lovers* of life are the *healers* of life because they're the *believers* of life.

Six-Sensory Practice

This week, feed your soul. Focus on what makes you content and fills you with a sense of satisfaction. Once you identify what brings you joy, seek to indulge in it every day. The more you nurture your spirit, the more attractive to others your energy will be, drawing to you all you need. Stop being too responsible, and make room to have more sweet, soul-soothing moments. See how different life feels when you feed your soul and how differently people act toward you.

Just like the song from *The Sound of Music,* name your favorite things. It will change your vibration and leave you feeling lighter. The entire world loves a lover, so this week, I encourage you to be a lover of life—sit down at the banquet, feast, and *enjoy!*

SIX-SENSORY WISDOM:

Feed your spirit.

SECRET #24
KNOW THAT THERE'S ALWAYS A SOLUTION

You can tell the difference between five-sensory and six-sensory people by how they view the world. Five-sensory people, peering through the viewfinder of the ego, look at the surface of life and see obstacles. Intuitives, coming from the soul, gaze at life and only see opportunities to grow.

Take, for example, Mary, who worked for a major airline as a flight attendant. Ever since deregulation in 1979, she was told that her company was going to disappear off the face of the earth and she'd be losing her job any day. For the next *11 years*, she fretted, fussed, and mentally rehearsed being unemployed until she convinced herself that she was a bag lady waiting to happen. Mary made herself sick with worry—never mind that the airline continued to fly, and that she never missed a day of work or a paycheck. She spent all those years suffering, only to end up having another airline merge with her employer, which stabilized her job and gave her a substantial raise. Not only was all that anxiety a waste, it actually ruined her health.

Neil, Mary's six-sensory co-worker, viewed the instability much differently. Not wanting to be at the mercy of things outside his control, he turned the situation into an opportunity by using his days off to learn the upholstery trade. Over the next 11 years, between flights Neil worked as a freelance upholsterer in his home studio, perfecting his skills and gaining clients and a good reputation by leaps and bounds. When the airline merger came through, Neil was able to switch to working part-time, which allowed him travel benefits and left him free to continue to develop his own business. Today, he's creatively *and* financially comfortable, and he's his own boss to boot.

The reason I'm so familiar with this six-sensory flight attendant is because he's my brother. Even though he and Mary both started in the same boat (so to speak), while all Mary could see were problems, Neil focused on solutions. When we were growing up in a six-sensory home, our mother emphasized that there was a solution to every problem, and it was up to our sixth sense to discover it, as if it were a game. She often said that uncovering solutions was her favorite sport in life. Neil simply put that lesson to work.

Part of being intuitive means that you take the raw material life gives you and you use your creative ability to transform it into gold. My teachers taught me that when an obstacle appears in our life, it's the Universe's way of redirecting us closer to our heart's desire.

For example, my client Matt was a particularly entrenched five-sensory being who viewed life as being against him. When the stock market crashed in 1987, he lost $200,000 in his retirement portfolio, which had taken him more than 25 years to build. The loss almost gave him a heart attack. "Why did my broker do this to me?" Matt lamented over and over again. Never mind that the entire country, and possibly the world, had suffered the same financial setback—he took it personally.

Matt failed to see what his six-sensory wife knew: They were living beyond their means. It was time to downsize, something Matt had resisted. The couple sold their home in Los Angeles and relocated to a simpler dwelling in a small town. Life was cheaper and easier, and the stress was significantly lower. Both Matt and his wife were far happier, and his financial concerns eased greatly. In the meantime, the market crept back up, and in less than two years their fiscal picture was better than ever, and the quality of their life had vastly improved. Matt still doesn't realize the gift he received; to this day, he dwells on the money he lost back in 1987.

Six-sensory people see any change of plans or unexpected setbacks as a time to grow, even when the upsets are painful. Kathy, a discontented financial consultant in New York, was on her way to an appointment at the World Trade Center on September 11, 2001. Realizing that she was a bit early, she stopped across the street for a cup of coffee, thus missing the terrorist attacks by minutes. The devastation and deep depression she felt in the aftermath eventually gave way to an inspiration and creativity she'd never felt before.

Kathy's life was lonely and had lacked meaning before the 9/11 tragedy, as most of her time was spent in the sole pursuit of helping rich people make more money. But since that tragic day, she's perceived being spared from death as a gift from God. She's since rerouted her talents into a more soulful pursuit of fund-raising for nonprofit organizations that work toward healing rage, racism, and abuse. While many of her nonpsychic friends are still struggling to regain their footing, she's never felt more focused and full of determination to make a difference in the world. The disaster knocked her out of her five-sensory point of view and opened her heart and mind to a six-sensory, soul-based life.

On a more personal scale, Karen and John also crossed the bridge from five-sensory to six-sensory living after the tragic loss of their three-year-old daughter, Haley, to cancer. Prior to their little girl's death, both Karen and John were strictly five-sensory, living a superficial, consumption-oriented life, adoring Haley but loathing each other. When Haley got sick, the family was thrown into chaos, but Karen's dormant psychic sense jumped into high gear. She knew in her heart that Haley wasn't going to make it, although they tried everything medically possible to keep her physically alive. Karen spent the limited time they had together loving and appreciating Haley in every way. Her immature priorities gave way to learning to love without condition, and despite the searing pain she felt, she recognized the gift her daughter's dying offered. For the first time in her life, Karen was living from her heart.

John had more trouble, for he felt hurt, betrayed, angry, and secretly responsible for his daughter's death. In his hopelessness, he pushed Karen away—until she asked for a divorce. Stunned, John realized how controlling, angry, and selfish he'd been. And he saw even more devastating loss on the horizon with Karen's leaving, so he reluctantly began to open his heart. This led the couple to completely disassemble their old life, including ending their careers, selling their home, relocating to a new town, and getting some major counseling. They not only salvaged their marriage, but John began the work of creating a life with meaning. "The gift in Haley's death," he said, "is that I was able to find my way back to living."

Your heart-based knowledge helps you navigate life's obstacles with grace. You'll never be able to completely eliminate challenges, because they're the fuel for our spiritual growth—but what the sixth sense does is wake you up to what's important. It gives you the insight and creative and psychic stamina to stay faithful to your soul's growth and to recognize that all challenges are only secret highways to learning to love without condition.

Five-sensory people often don't recognize that Divine Wisdom is always operating on their behalf. For instance, a five-sensory client of mine once called me, feeling distraught because a snowstorm had closed the roads to the airport, causing her and her family to be snowed in at a ski resort. Frustrated that everyone was off schedule and life was marching on without them, my client forgot that normally, she, her husband, and their college-aged kids were all over the map and rarely get together. Consequently, she missed out on enjoying the gift of two extra days with her family.

However, being six-sensory is more than being an optimist or having a good attitude. It means trusting that life is unfolding as it should, and it's always leading you directly toward your true path. A six-sensory being isn't merely willing to look on the bright side of difficult things, but rather recognizes that the obstacles we face or the changes we encounter are the Universe's way of prodding us to grow (even if it does seem unbearable at times). Without them, we could possibly miss life altogether. Five-sensory people see life's challenges as red lights and burdens, while six-sensory people see them as green lights and personal development.

My mother, one of my favorite six-sensory people of all time, taught me that life never stops us—it just gives us a reason to come up with a better idea. We intuitives love to come up with better ideas because we know that we have the full support and assistance of the Universe. When I think of the men I could have married, the career choices I could have made, or the commitments and ideas I might have pursued save for the Universe's interference, I'm extremely grateful to have been rerouted—and for knowing in my heart that despite my life's obstacles and disappointments, I was always being directed toward my highest and most creative good.

Six-Sensory Practice

This week, view every inconvenience, disappointment, challenge, and upset as an invitation to live a higher way. Embrace the opportunity, and ask your Higher Self to guide you to the gift it holds.

Review past problems with the same scrutiny, and list the positive things that have arisen from difficulties. Where were you inspired to try new ideas? When were you spared from making mistakes? How did you discover the gifts that arise from challenge? Whether it's a traffic jam, a missed appointment, a cancelled date, a client who rejects you, or even an illness or death, somewhere there are new directions, new opportunities, new lessons, and new solutions. Are you able to see them? Do you want to? Are you willing to stop being a victim of life and start being an inventor? Stop pushing upstream—surrender instead, and learn to go with the flow. And know that for every problem, there is a solution. You just need to undertake the sport of finding it.

SIX-SENSORY WISDOM:

Know that there's gold in them thar hills.

PART VII

Take the High Road

By now it should be crystal clear that following five-sensory, ego-based rules is a dead-end street. Even though the ego thinks it's protecting you by running all this interference, it isn't. The key to freedom is to get around the ego, which by this time is probably running scared.

So let's bring out the big guns—it's time to push to the six-sensory world and let spiritual law take over. Otherwise your very tenacious ego can keep you going in circles forever, stuck in what I call the "Yeah, but" syndrome: "Yeah, but what if I make a mistake? Yeah, but what if my feelings are wrong? Yeah, but what if people think I'm an idiot for being intuitive?" Yeah, but . . . if you keep going along this way, you'll never trust what you've worked so hard to connect with—your spirit.

One of my favorite strategies for dismantling the blocks to the sixth sense is to engage my subconscious mind, which follows spiritual law, and carry it over to the cause of spiritual freedom and life in the flow. It's amazingly simple: I just direct my subconscious to override any belief coming from my ego. In other words, rather than deconstructing each false belief, distorted emotion, or self-limiting behavior the ego puts in my way, which can be time-consuming and endless, I actually activate my subconscious mind to simply step over these blocks.

One day during a heated argument with my husband, Patrick, I stormed out of the room, intending to say, "If you don't stop, I'm leaving you." What came out of my mouth instead was, "I wish you would stop, and I love you." It surprised both of us and immediately ended the argument.

Directing your subconscious mind to bypass the ego's resistance makes life a lot easier—especially if your ego forces you to jump to conclusions, make errors in judgment, ignore your intuition, or any number of sabotaging tricks—because it will keep you on course in spite of yourself. By overriding ego-based beliefs that cut off your sixth sense, you'll deflect any self-sabotaging behavior, which leads to amazing and sometimes amusing results. When you invite your Higher Self to take over the reins of your life, it will, even if your ego has other ideas. Programming your subconscious mind to listen to and respond only to your Higher Self will keep you faithful to your vibes—and to what you really want—often in a most hilarious way. You surrender completely to Divine Will, get out of your own way, and let God's wisdom take over.

This is what I had in mind when I suggested to my client Roseanne that she direct her subconscious mind to listen only to her Higher Self. Roseanne's ego was making a terrible mess of things, and her latest dilemma concerned whether or not she should continue dating a certain man. "I don't know what to do about this guy," she said. "He's a freelance writer, which scares me because that means his income isn't stable. He's been engaged twice and broke it off both times, which means he's noncommittal. He dresses like a slob, which embarrasses me. I don't know what to do. I like him, but so many things are wrong."

Instead of trying to alleviate her fears, which were relentless and a festival for her ego, I said that Roseanne should see that her ego was trying to sabotage her, and she should sidestep the interference by plugging directly in to her Higher Self for guidance. It would have been fruitless to give her any other advice because her ego would have just dished up an even larger plate of confusion (which was its modus operandi for keeping her stuck). To address her worries would have gotten us nowhere—

it was far more helpful for her to learn how to clear the plate of drivel coming from her ego. That would open the way for her to trust her sixth sense and not depend on mine to guide her toward the right answer.

After I told her all this, Roseanne asked me, wide-eyed, "Do you mean *I* can do that—I don't need you?"

"Yes."

"And I can trust what I get? You know I don't trust anything."

"Yes."

"Okay. What do I do?"

"Say 'I instruct my subconscious mind to only follow my Higher Self in spite of what my mind says.'"

"That's it?"

"That's it."

I told Roseanne to repeat the sentence I gave her over and over again for the next few weeks, especially when she worried or was caught up in trying to figure things out. I told her to repeat it instead of calling friends and agonizing over what to do. She was skeptical, but I assured her that it would work a miracle and give her the answers she was looking for. So she did what I suggested. At first, she didn't feel any difference in her life. Then one night, as Roseanne and her boyfriend were trying to decide what to do, going around and around and wasting time like always, her boyfriend finally pleaded, "Just tell me what you really want to do more than anything else. I'll do whatever you want."

She started to say, "I'd really like to go to a movie," but what came out was, "I'd just like to get married so that I don't have to think about whether or not you're the right one anymore."

In disbelief, he asked, "What did you say?"

Roseanne's Higher Self had taken over, so she continued to speak. "I know in my heart that you're right for me," she admitted, "and I don't want to screw it up with my fears like I do everything else."

He hesitated for a second, dumbfounded by her unexpected disclosure, then said, "Then that's what we should do."

And off they went and eloped, just like that. Before that moment, Roseanne had never done a spontaneous thing in her life, let alone trusted her heart and intuition, because she was such a slave to her ego's rules. Yet in that instant, she was liberated, and she enjoyed her truth. Rewriting the rules and rewiring herself to her Higher Self freed her. Although she still wrestles with her ego to this day, it no longer stops her from trusting her vibes. And she's still learning how to be comfortable with spiritual law, but her allegiance has permanently shifted away from her ego. (I'm happy to report that, six years later, Roseanne and her husband are still happily married and getting ready to have their first baby.)

Directing your subconscious mind to bypass the ego is not as odd as it sounds. You do this anytime you focus on something, or repeat anything over and over, for a few days. We call that developing a habit. That habit imprints your subconscious mind, and the behavior starts occurring on its own.

When a newborn baby arrives, it knows nothing about taking care of itself. Yet in five to seven days it learns how to find and suck its fingers or thumb for comfort—that's how quickly it has programmed its subconscious to create the habit of comforting itself. It takes about the same amount of time to develop *any* grown-up habit. So if you spend seven days programming your subconscious mind, it will override blocks to your psychic sense by your ego and keep you faithful to your vibes.

For example, Patrick and I were flying home late one Sunday evening from Albuquerque via St. Louis on standby. When we arrived at the connecting flight's gate, we were dismayed to be told that there were 35 passengers ahead of us and the flight was already full, so our chances of getting on were zero.

Patrick thought that we should get a hotel room and try the next day. This made sense to me, since it was late and there was no use standing around. Except my body wouldn't budge. He started to walk away, but I sat firmly in my chair. The flight filled up, a few standby passengers were called, and the attendant said, "That's it, folks. Try again tomorrow."

All the remaining passengers had gone—only I remained.

"Let's go," said Patrick impatiently. I said okay, but my body still wouldn't budge, even though the plane was taxiing away. Looking very annoyed, Patrick asked, "Well, are you coming?"

I said yes, but I still sat there. I wondered what on earth was the matter with me. Just then the plane started returning to the terminal, and the agent disappeared behind the door. Thirty seconds later, she got off with three passengers following her, two adults and a five-year-old child. She looked at us and said, "We made a mistake—there were only two seats left, and these people didn't want to split up."

Seeing that all the other passengers had left, she said, "I guess it's your lucky night." We hurriedly boarded, and we were back in Chicago an hour later. I was extremely grateful to my Higher Self that night because I wanted to leave and it wouldn't let me. It kept me right in that chair despite myself. *Thank you, God,* I thought as I snuggled into my comfortable bed just a few hours later.

THE GREAT THING ABOUT PROGRAMMING your subconscious mind to listen only to your Higher Self and not your ego is that it simplifies following your vibes and being six-sensory in a five-sensory world. When you invite your Higher Self to be in charge of your life, you don't have to worry about goofing up and staying stuck in your ego, even if you want to. Your Higher Self can override your negative ego patterns if you ask it to, and then living a six-sensory life will become second nature.

Interestingly, many people do this already in part (although they may not realize it) when they spend time on those pursuits that move them into their hearts. For example, I have a friend who's a singer-songwriter. He's never taken a formal lesson in his life, yet he composes, sings, and plays beautiful, soulful ballads like a master. When asked where he gets his inspiration from, he responds, "I honestly don't know. I don't ever think about the songs—they simply show up."

Patrick has that same connection to his Higher Self when it comes to cooking. He's a food genius, but most of the time he can't tell you how he prepared something or what inspired him—

it's automatic. "I just do this and that and don't even know what I did or why, but it works," he says.

The Higher Self is in charge anytime you express yourself through your talents. When you invite your Higher Self to run your life, you clear away the obstacles that your ego set up, or you simply hurdle over them. You stop thinking; you just know. This is how I do intuitive readings for clients. I, Sonia, the ego, don't do them—I allow my Higher Self to come in and do the work because it's much easier. I don't even think about what I say until I say it, but I trust that my Higher Self knows what I'm doing. So I get out of the way and let it happen. There are days when I don't even remember what I said, but it makes perfect sense to my clients.

Perhaps you too already have your Higher Self running some part of your life. If so, just do it, whatever it is, and don't think about it too much. The best part about giving your Higher Self executive status to override any resistance to your psychic sense is that it makes the transition to living in a higher way much easier. It's a lot less taxing to your emotional system, takes less energy, brings about positive outcomes, and gives your brain a break. I think it even makes you younger.

The way to influence your subconscious mind to cooperate and shift its alliances from ego to Higher Self is through repetition and consistency, so repeat your intention over and over until it clicks. The simpler the mantra, the better. Mine is: "My Higher Self rules." And it does. Yours can, too.

Six-Sensory Practice

This week, repeat often: "Subconscious mind, my Higher Self is the boss." Write this phrase on slips of paper and tape them in prominent places throughout your home and workspace as a constant visual reminder. And the minute you find yourself worrying, struggling, or questioning over what to do, again repeat: "Higher Self, take over."

Make a note of all those areas where your Higher Self is already on the job. How do things flow in these areas? Do you like it? Finally, add a little music to your mantra, singing it to yourself rather than just saying it. The subconscious mind responds best to music, so if you sing it, it will stick.

SIX-SENSORY WISDOM:

Let your Higher Self lead.

SECRET #26

One of the great discoveries you'll make when you open your intuitive channel is clairvoyance (or "clear vision"). But before you can access this extrasensory perception, you must first learn to see what's right in front of your nose, not just what you *want* to see. Most five-sensory people are casual and careless in their observations of the world—as they quickly glance at who and what is around them, their prideful egos draw rapid and erroneous conclusions that lead to all sorts of misunderstandings and failed opportunities.

The basis of clairvoyance is to study what's really present without projection, distortion, sentimentality, or fear. In other words, what's really there? This kind of lucid and objective point of view invites you to move to a deeper level of seeing; it engages you to look at life from your spirit, rather than looking from your ego. The more accurately you study the world and the people around you, the deeper and more profound your insights will be.

If you want to be clairvoyant, you must first observe every detail, every muscle twitch, every habit and behavior as the footing for finding out who another person is on a deeper plane. Not only must you be astute in your perceptions, but you must also look past a person's protective facade and defensive posturing and to their true spirit. This must be done from your authentic spirit, not from a defensive or judgmental viewpoint. Look for what's real in others, from a place that's real in you.

Poor observation, or ego observation, is almost always to blame for our problems with others. This is especially true when we're hurt or betrayed by someone and feel that they caused us harm on purpose. For example, I spoke with a client recently who was outraged that her husband had left her and run off with his secretary. She couldn't believe that he could do this to her—yet, if she'd been objective and had studied the situation more accurately from her spirit, she would have remembered that he'd left two previous marriages for other women (my client being the new woman herself at one time). She also would have realized that her husband had long withdrawn from being intimate with her, he'd spoken often of feeling depressed, and he suffered from several addictions that prevented him from being honest. Amazingly, she didn't see any of these signs as spelling doom for her marriage, although I believe that she didn't see trouble coming because she didn't want to, yet then felt victimized when it did.

I had another client who, whenever she looked at an overweight person, told herself that he or she must be lazy. She ultimately developed an intense dislike of heavy people, which became a problem at work, where she had to team with several large-sized co-workers. Her projections prevented her from being open to their talent and contributions, and she assumed that she needed to work alone, shutting out any receptivity to collaboration with her fellow employees, who, in turn, felt ignored and frustrated. Ultimately hating her control, her team members quit, one after the other, and she *did* end up doing all the work. She never saw the problem until one of the "lazy" ones started an advertising agency, and in the first year won two industry awards of excellence. My client was forced into taking a second look.

Just as our inability to see the truth harms us when we project negative filters, it can also backfire just as easily when we project positive ones that are no more accurate. For example, a student of mine ran a busy design firm. She was so desperate for a personal assistant that she called a temp agency, who sent over a woman who seemed very nice. Grateful for the help, my student latched on to this woman with a vengeance, placing full confidence in her before she'd properly scrutinized her. My student gave her house keys, bank deposits, and even the authority to sign checks, all the while singing her praises.

This went on for three months, until one day my student's bank called to tell her that she was overdrawn by $20,000. She called her assistant, who admitted that she took it, adding, "You'll never be able to find me to return the money. Besides, you'll get over it."

Stunned and hurt, my student asked, "But why? I was so good to you."

She answered, "Because you're rich and don't need it, and I do," and hung up. Reeling from disbelief, my student called the temp agency to find out more about this woman in order to press charges, only to discover that it was no longer in business. Her carelessness was an expensive and painful lesson.

Not only do we bury our heads in the sand when it comes to life, we also tend to do this when we fall in love. I remember once when a friend of mine called to tell me that she was madly in love and wanted me to meet her great new boyfriend. When I asked what he was like, she gushed that he was charming and charismatic, and best of all, he looked exactly like Richard Gere.

When I met this man, he was extremely rude, barking into his cell phone throughout dinner, eating with his mouth open and using his fingers, and talking over everyone at the table. As for looking like Richard Gere . . . all I could see was Pee-wee Herman on a bad hair day. Oh well, my friend and I clearly weren't perceiving the same thing.

Emotional blinders and assumptions are two poor habits that prevent you from gaining a clear view of what *is*, and without an accurate view, you risk having a poor understanding of another and making the wrong choices. Lazy, ego-based observation may very well be at the root of most of your life's problems. If you'd only take the time to see the situation correctly from a spiritual perspective before you draw your conclusions or make your plans, you could prevent many mistakes and open up to brilliant insights.

My teacher Dr. Tully told me, "Never assume you know any-one completely." Doing so projects your ideas, your assump-tions, and your limitations onto them. The more you practice seeing someone for who they really are, the closer you come to knowing and understanding that person. The way you look at the world is a habit, so you may be looking through some very strong filters. Your beliefs, judgments, biases, and patterns will keep you from seeing the truth if you let them. As I've repeat-edly stated, the truth derails the ego, which doesn't want to give up the upper hand, so it runs interference to keep you from reality. Don't let it. There are ugly and painful conditions out there and in us, and we often fear that seeing them is more than we can bear. But until we see them, we can't heal them. Denial as a form of protection doesn't work. I've never known a case where ignoring the truth has served anyone. Have you? And yet, I've been humbled to see how healing and powerful accurate insight can be.

To activate your higher sense of clairvoyance, look deeply into people's hearts. Recognize that underneath the facade, each of us is simply a vulnerable human being who feels insecure and only wants to be loved and accepted. With that in mind, observe with neutral curiosity how others go about getting that love and acceptance. Watch and listen long and hard with an interested perspective rather than a closed one, and you'll see how amus-ing, lovable, and similar we all are. In other words, follow spiri-tual law, not ego-based law, when observing the world.

Ninety-nine percent of your problems could be avoided if you'd just activate your clear vision and look at your life and oth-ers more honestly and objectively. To do so invites you to be rea-sonable. As my teacher Charlie once told me, "Sonia, your sixth sense is really a keen sense of the obvious." I agree. The more you want to see the truth, the more profound your vision will become. Clairvoyance develops gradually from accurate observation and solid reason, so the more you objectively observe what's real at the moment, the more you'll intuitively see what will be real in the future. The more you're receptive to the truth about a per-son, the more their truth will emerge.

To observe others accurately is to be more interested *in* them than in how you appear *to* them. If you're willing to shift your focus from yourself and place it squarely on knowing all you can about others, you'll see all you're looking for. The key to looking into others and understanding them on the deepest level is to look with loving neutrality, not with judgment or suspicion. The more you practice looking at life on this level, the more you'll activate your higher vision: clairvoyance.

With clairvoyance, not only will you see what's on the physical plane, but you'll see what's on the energy plane as well. This leads to compassion, understanding, and love, which then leads to creative and positive outcomes and prevents misunderstandings and mistakes.

Six-Sensory Practice

For the next week, look at life on its deepest level. Study other people with an open and objective mind and a loving heart. Pay attention to what's in front of you: Study facial expressions and body language. Be interested in others instead of worrying about how you appear to them. Be sure to look past people's facades, and search for deeper clarity and insight. Ask yourself if you're seeing their greatest fears, strengths, talents, or secret hearts' desires. Look for details you haven't noticed before. Practice this particularly with people you look at every day. What do you see that you've never seen before?

Be willing to look at others without judging, projecting, or telling yourself a story about them. Be neutral, as if you were looking at a beautiful landscape. Simply observe and learn.

SIX-SENSORY WISDOM:

Look past appearances.

SECRET #27

LOOK DIVINE

To look at the world from the vantage point of your soul is to look from the Divine part of yourself, which means that you'll see the world through the eyes of God. Can you imagine this? Looking at the world from this perspective would cleanse you of bias, projection, and distortion, for God sees through obstacles and defenses set up by you and others. Not only would this shift in perception allow you to accurately view the physical world, it would also give you instant access to the deeper, energetic body of others. When your soul looks into the souls of others, you'll be amazed at how much more beauty you'll see in people.

This was not the case with Penny, who came to see me because she was sick and tired of Marshall, her "freeloading husband." Marshall hadn't held a consistent job during the ten years of their marriage, even though Penny had found him several jobs in the computer industry. She ranted and raved about how "lazy, irresponsible, childish, unfocused, and burdensome" he was, and how he "just wanted to play with his tools," and until he got a real paycheck, she couldn't fulfill her deepest desire to have children. She was nearly blind with rage over his unproductive life and wanted me to help her "make something out of the louse."

When I intuitively viewed Marshall, however, I didn't see anything resembling Penny's description. I saw a frustrated man who was very gifted with his hands and had several potential artistic and healing talents that, if developed, would be quite valuable. He just wasn't ambitious in the same material way that his wife was. Although I could see that they could teach each other about life, until they appreciated each other's spirits it would be very difficult.

When I looked at this man from the eyes of God, as my clairvoyant training had taught me, I saw his hands glowing as if they were made of gold. Searching more deeply, I perceived talent as a massage therapist and a sculptor, both of which would channel enormous healing and would fulfill his purpose. I shared these observations with Penny, but she scoffed. "Yeah, he says the same thing," she said. "That something with art or massage therapy is what he wants to do, and, hey, so would I! But that won't pay the rent. He needs a real job working a computer, or selling something like I do."

Penny's comments sadly revealed her shortsightedness, not her husband's. Because she was so five-sensory, materialistic, and unconscious of the soul, she couldn't perceive that Marshall's beautiful healing and artistic talents had any value. And because she couldn't see his talents through her eyes, she mistakenly decided they weren't real.

I suggested that perhaps the problem was hers, not his, and that if she could just see and value who he really was—an artist and healer—and support that, he could get on with his work and make a decent living, and they could have the family she wanted. It was a matter of first things first.

"You mean actually *encourage* the nonsense he does? You're as unrealistic as he is," she said.

Sadly, Penny never did see Marshall through God's eyes—she continued to indict him as a dreamer and a freeloader, and they soon divorced. Five years later, Marshall came to see me for a reading. After the divorce, he'd gone to massage school, and at the same time, he started sculpting in earnest. He married a woman he'd met at school who recognized, appreciated, and truly loved his talents. With her support, he began a private practice in massage therapy and eventually found an agent to represent his art.

The first year he sold six sculptures (from $2,000 to $7,000 each), and had a piece accepted by a small museum in Canada. I wasn't surprised—his talent was always there, and with the support of someone who shared his vision, it blossomed and found its way into the world.

Marshall's second wife was a six-sensory being whose nurturing view activated his potential, like water in a neglected garden. Rather than being frustrated in not seeing what she wanted to see in him (like Penny did), his second wife was enamored of seeing what he could become, and with her Divine view, he became that over time.

Looking through the eyes of God does far more than merely soften our view and motivate us to look for the good in people. It gives us the potential to see past appearances to the energy body itself, which can prove to be lifesaving. For example, my client Beth made a spiritual decision several years ago to look at the world and everyone in it through God's eyes, and immediately her perceptions began to reveal incredible things. One day she was sitting in a board meeting when her intuition flashed an image of the company president—a relatively young guy who was seemingly healthy—having a heart attack. She blinked several times and tried to shake the image, but it persisted. She wasn't sure what to do, but when the meeting was over, she took a chance and approached him, very cautiously asking how he was feeling.

"Fine," he responded. "Why?"

She hesitated, then shared her vision with him, although she toned it down a lot. He laughed and assured her that he really was okay, but added, "I'll tell you what—just to respect your input, I'll take it as a sign to get a checkup soon."

Three weeks later, Beth received a memo summoning her to the president's office. As she entered, she noticed that he looked quite shaken. "Just because I'm a superstitious guy and felt that your comment was an omen, I followed it and got a physical," he said. "It seems that I have some major heart blockages that I wasn't aware of. I'm going in for surgery this week. Do you know that you may have spared me a heart attack or worse?"

Beth was astounded and grateful that she'd had the courage to share what she saw with her boss. So was he.

Looking through the eyes of God improves your vision and invites you, as a higher conscious being, to see the truth about others and yourself on both a physical and energy plane. "The minute I began to look through my soul's eyes, the world shifted dramatically," said Jim, a student who was taking my psychic-awakening course. "Before I shifted my perception, I realized that I wasn't really looking into people at all. Instead, I was casting sideways glances at others and then making up scary stories about them based upon my insecure and inaccurate observations. When I decided to look with the eyes of God, as you suggested, life brightened up and people suddenly became quite beautiful. I wasn't merely looking at physical appearances anymore (which, by the way, I did enjoy)—I began to look into their eyes and could actually see their souls. This recognition was so healing, profound, and moving that no matter who I looked at, my heart burst wide open. I'm embarrassed to admit that at times I even felt like crying," he said. "Not only do I now see the soul of a person, but when I look, I actually get who he or she is. I can't explain this in words, but on some organic level I understand others like I never did before."

Jim's experience is typical of what life looks like to us six-sensory people. Our vision raises an octave and we have more capacity to perceive the richness and complexity of the objects and people around us. We sense, and ultimately see, both physical bodies and energy bodies, including their auras.

My client Miriam had an exciting surprise when she decided to view the world with her soul eyes: "I saw an incredible violet light radiating from the tree in my backyard, pulsating very gently, but full of energy. It actually scared me," she said. "Then I looked at my garden and an array of similar light bounced around the tops of my flowers. Always being a nature lover, I've appreciated the beauty of the physical world, but with this change in my perspective, life became so much more intensely beautiful that it moved me to tears. *How could I have missed this,* I wondered. It's so awesome."

Looking through the eyes of God enables you to perceive and comprehend everything on a much deeper level than mere intellectual viewing can because your soul eyes respond to a different vibration, one your physical eyes don't register. It also invites you to see the shape of the world to come, which reveals what creations will unfold and what your soul's intentions will express.

One of the most powerful ways to use your soul's eyes is to become what my writing mentor and friend, Julia Cameron, introduced to me as *believing eyes*. Several years ago, I wanted to write a book on awakening the sixth sense, but I doubted my ability to write. Julia, on the other hand, had no doubt that I could do it, and for the next six months she chose to see me as a gifted and prolific writer. Her steady gaze, full of conviction and faith, reflected unwaveringly back to me, eventually resonated in *my* view of myself, until I too had no doubt. At the end of the six months, basking in the gaze of those believing eyes, I'd written my first book, *The Psychic Pathway*. I'm absolutely convinced that Julia's view of me as a writer was the reason I became one. Without her ability to see me as I wanted to be seen, I wonder if my dream would still be merely that—a dream.

The clients I've told this story to have said that I'm so lucky to have had believing eyes from Julia, but they don't have such luck, so they're stuck. It's true that I *was* lucky, and I'm deeply grateful. But ever since receiving Julia's gift, I've studied believing eyes. I've found that in order to attract them, you must first *become* believing eyes by choosing to see and believe in other people's heart's desires and future creations, being the faithkeeper until they develop faith in themselves.

While Julia held the vision for me as a writer, I held a vision for her as a clairvoyant. It was our reciprocal view arising from our souls that gave birth to my book and the beginning of her clairvoyant and psychic life. So see the difference you'd *like to see* in the world. You have a choice: You can either look at the world from an unconscious, superficial, five-sensory point of view—focusing on flaws, perceiving separation through judgment and fear, and scaring yourself to death; or, using your sixth sense, you can seek to see the soul in others, to recognize and to appreciate the beauty in everyone and have compassion for all.

You can also choose to see people as they appear in the moment, which your five senses do, or you can choose to see the spirit in people and what they're becoming on a soul level, which the sixth sense does. When I met my husband, for instance, he lived in an old warehouse, and his sole possessions were an old bike and a pair of skis. Those who knew him warned me to stay away because he was flaky and noncommittal—but that wasn't what my soul saw. I saw a soul mate, a fellow adventurer, and a faithful and creative companion. I chose what I saw over what appeared and what others told me was there.

Twenty-one years and two children later, I can happily say that what I saw on a soul level proved to be absolutely true. Patrick has been a faithful, creative, loving companion; a great father; a good teacher; a real adventurer; and my best friend. Of course we've had our challenges and they've been difficult, as they tend to be when two people work to create a deep, intimate relationship. But through it all, we've held the same vision of our life together, and the growth and benefits I've received from our marriage have proven to be one of my life's greatest gifts.

So, remember that when you look from the soul, you look through God's eyes, and God has 20/20 vision in hindsight *and* foresight.

Six-Sensory Practice

This week, view the world through God's eyes, especially in situations where you don't like what you see. What difference does this change in perception bring about? Are you able to see more accurately or more deeply with your soul eyes? What major insights, shifts, and discoveries are revealed?

Choose at least one person for whom you can become believing eyes and who can serve as yours. Start reflecting to one another the *you* each of you wants to become. Next, look for one beautiful thing in every person you deal with and say so—don't give false compliments or empty flattery. Then do this with yourself every morning. It's easy to dismiss this part of the practice, but when you can look at yourself with genuine appreciation, you'll know that you've made the transition from ego-based critical rules to spirit-based loving law.

SIX-SENSORY WISDOM:

See God within everything.

PART VIII

The Art of Six-Sensory Living

SECRET #28

LAUGHING MATTERS

The more lighthearted you are, the easier it is to live in a higher way. You see, a light heart raises your vibration to a higher frequency and automatically tunes you in to your sixth sense. This then opens you to receive healing vibes, guidance, and insight from your Higher Self and spirit helpers.

One of the best ways to lighten up is to simply laugh—a lot—for this instantly raises your energy, opens your heart, and elevates your vibration effortlessly. Laughing not only lifts your awareness to a clear and high frequency, but it also cleanses and repairs your aura, heals your spirit, and energizes your soul. When you laugh hard, you lose yourself and merge with the Divine, which releases you from fear's grip, catapults you into a higher perspective, and connects you to the eternal. Nothing has control over you if you can laugh at it.

Laughter provides a door to your soul so that you forget your troubles, even for a moment; and you clear away negativity, confusion, and mind chatter. In my studies years ago, I learned that "laughter chases the devil away"—the devil being any illusion, distortion, and confusion that throws you into doubt, scares you, or causes you to question your basic worth and goodness.

Taking yourself too seriously is an obstacle to trusting your vibes. Your serious, or intellectual, self is your ego posturing again, relentlessly trying to stay in charge;

while your lighthearted, more playful self is your spirit allowing the Universe to run the show. This doesn't mean that what your spirit concerns itself with isn't important—it's that you don't want to confuse what's profound with what's serious. The profound teaches, heals, and makes your capacity to love yourself and others more compassionate; the serious is usually just a position to protect your ego from feeling vulnerable. To the spirit, nothing is serious enough to take away your light heart, not even death. Of course you can have somber moments, for these are aspects of your soul, but your self-important moments require you to be on guard because they're just your ego parading around and blocking you from accessing your spirit.

This reminds me of a six-sensory workshop I recently taught at the Omega Institute in New York. The class was taking themselves way too seriously for their own good; consequently, most of the students were having no luck tapping in to their sixth sense. To help them move out of this blocked state, I encouraged them to make each other laugh. At first they thought this was a stupid idea that challenged their sense of importance, but eventually they gave in and tried.

They were a little rusty and not very funny in the beginning, but eventually the participants got with it and became more amusing. Some started playing trombone with their armpits, while others began crossing their eyes and making funny faces. They pretended to be animals, hopping on one foot, making silly noises, and acting like a group of crazed kindergartners. The longer they tried, the funnier they became, until genuine hilarity caught on, which made them laugh even more. For 15 minutes, everyone was so consumed with lighthearted silliness that I could barely get them to stop.

I invited the group to try their psychic muscles again and use their sixth sense with each another. Much to their amazement, in this freer, lighthearted state of mind they were able to see into each other's lives and accurately discern things they couldn't have known before. They could describe homes, jobs, secret heart's desires, travel plans, and even great loves, although they were strangers to one another. No one remained blocked, and even the most doubting Thomases were surprised at how much a little humor let them better know the people around them.

Laughter connects you to the big picture and expands your view, as Charlie Goodman, my first intuitive teacher, taught me. Charlie introduced laughter as a door to my sixth sense, and when I studied with him, he sometimes made me laugh so hard that tears ran down my cheeks. "No matter what you see or feel," he'd emphasize, "always keep a sense of humor about it."

My mother, another of my great inspirations, agreed with him wholeheartedly. She'd say, "The situation may be critical, but it's never serious." I found that the more I looked for the humor in things, the more I saw Divine Spirit lending a guiding and humorous hand.

To be intuitive, we must cultivate our sense of humor and look for reasons to laugh everywhere. We become so self-absorbed and serious when it comes to our problems and melodramas that we disconnect from our deeper sense of who we are as beautiful souls—we withdraw from life instead of enjoying it. Laughter brings us back to ourselves and back to life.

WHAT MAKES YOU LAUGH? Find out, and indulge often. And if you're feeling depressed or don't even feel like smiling, try faking it. Believe it or not, this really works. For example, last summer when I was teaching in San Francisco, a 78-year-old man told me that he'd just spent a week at a wellness center where he and other seriously depressed people were treated by being asked to lie down on the floor and laugh for 30 minutes a day, even if they didn't feel like it. The instructors told them to fake it if they had to, but they were required to do it. This man couldn't explain why, but he soon began to feel much better. By the end of the week, he'd left behind a depressed and heavy heart that had plagued him ever since his divorce 15 years before. It's no wonder—laughing chases away the dark shadows of life and instantly raises our vibration to a more evolved, wholesome state. Faking it works because if we do it enough, the humor angels eventually show up and turn the real laughing gas (and healing) on.

In my intuitive practice, I've seen many people much too

serious in the name of spiritual growth, losing all humor, spontaneity, and joy because they think this work is "holy." My client Brenda, for instance, meditated for hours each day, ate only the most pure organic food, gave herself wheat-grass enemas every morning, and wrapped herself in every amulet, crystal, talisman, and titanium gadget she could get her hands on for purification and protection. In pursuit of her "holiness," she read books endlessly, attended countless workshops and lectures, and was a self-appointed expert on every New Age subject (which she felt she knew more about than her instructors did).

Yet for all her efforts, Brenda was one of the most humorless, bitter, and uncreative people I've ever known. She was so controlling that intuitively she had no connection to her Higher Self, her heart, her humor, or anything *really* spiritual. I suggested several times that she stop her incessant self-improvement and secret self-loathing and lighten up. Her efforts seemed excessive and silly, and I tried to get her to see the humor in them. She didn't. And she was insulted when I said that while life is important, she shouldn't be quite so serious. She stormed out of my office, dismissing me as wasting her time. Maybe I was, but she was also doing a good job of that on her own.

It's important not to fall into the same trap that Brenda did—that is, letting your ego trick you into believing that life is a struggle and being spiritual is the greatest struggle of all. *It isn't.* The higher way reveals that life's a joy and an adventure, and even though it may be scary at times, you always have help through your psychic sense.

Some people can't distinguish between the ego and the sixth sense. Here's the difference: Your spirit is relaxed, forgiving, and laughs a lot, especially at you and your own antics; and your ego is critical and controlling and rarely laughs at anything, especially itself. The soul gently requests and trusts, while the ego demands and is suspicious. The soul is light and easy and loves adventures; the ego can be harsh and heavy and gets stuck in the mud.

When I began to open my sixth sense, I was told to find something humorous every day for three months. The kind of humor I was to look for, however, was not sarcasm, which is passed off as humor but is really thinly disguised anger or cynicism. That's the opposite of believing in life. Instead, I was sent in search of the sweet, silly, ridiculous, and absurd in life. This opened my heart and helped me feel more compassion, tolerance, and affection for myself and for my fellow human beings.

I'm eternally grateful for that assignment because it permanently changed my point of view. Now I automatically look for the humor first, no matter how dark a situation may be. In doing so, I see the spirit in everyone and the light in everything, and I know that whatever obstacle I face, I'll get through it and learn.

My spiritual role models are those who are quick to smile and are generous and easy with their laughter. Thich Nhat Hanh, the Dalai Lama, Ram Dass, and my mom (to name a few) all laugh as easily as a babbling brook. When Mother Teresa was alive, she insisted that the nuns who worked in her home for the destitute and dying stop whatever they were doing and play for an hour every afternoon. This kept her helpers healthy and devoted and filled with joy and love as they tended the dying. If Mother Teresa and the Dalai Lama could laugh with their life challenges, then surely we can, too. Laughing doesn't diminish the importance of serious issues in our life—rather, it channels the wisdom to heal them.

Six-Sensory Practice

This week, laugh a lot. Look for the humor in things: Sing in the shower, create shampoo sculptures with your hair in the bathtub, make funny faces while brushing your teeth, read humorous books, rent comedies, go to a karaoke club with a friend and join in, call your best pal from grade school and reminisce, goof around with your kids, and play with your dog. In other words, get over your seriousness and let your hair down! Fake it if you have to, but do a good job of it. Don't worry if you look foolish— the more foolish you are, the more enlightened you'll feel.

Notice how laughter inspires you and activates your sixth sense. Be prepared for intuitive flashes of genius, bright ideas, unbelievable dreams, synchronicities, and the inner peace that will surely follow.

SIX-SENSORY WISDOM:

Remember: The situation is critical, but not serious.

SECRET #29

USE CRAYONS

Living a six-sensory life is an art, not a science, because it follows spiritual law (your knowing heart) and not ego-based law (your intellectual self). One of the most effective ways, therefore, to get on the bandwagon of higher living is to engage often in something artistic, something outside the box of your ego-thinking patterns. Creative endeavors lead you to a more soulful perspective, acting as psychic jumper cables to your intuitive self.

Many of my clients have reported having illuminating psychic inspirations when they've engaged in a creative project because they temporarily stop thinking and are just being. For example, Maureen said that when she and her granddaughter were finger-painting one evening, at first she was merely humoring the child, but Maureen soon got caught up in the project and lost herself in it. As she smeared away, laughing and having fun with the mess, Maureen suddenly realized where she'd placed some important papers that she'd been searching for weeks. She was able to retrieve them that night.

Ron was landscaping his yard, carefully laying out bulbs in a geometric pattern that he'd designed in his mind, when he got a hit to create labyrinths with flowers. He drew the idea, told people about it, and they loved it. Ron soon began selling the patterns, and this business eventually allowed him to quit the warehouse job he'd wanted to leave for years.

As a newly divorced mother, Melinda was feeling very lonely and isolated. Not knowing how to move on, she enrolled in a watercolor-painting class. In the third session, she got a vibe to contact her best friend from high school, whom she hadn't spoken to in 30 years. Following her hunch, Melinda hunted her old friend down, and they had coffee the next month. Upon learning that Melinda was single, her friend said, "You should meet my neighbor—he's single and a nice guy." A blind date was arranged, and the chemistry worked: After less than a year, Melinda and this man were married.

Sometimes people back away from artful expression because they feel that they aren't worthy of frolicking on that playground. They're afraid to take creative risks because they were discouraged from freely expressing themselves when they were young. These people need to realize that art and vibes are soul mates, both natural expressions of the Divine Spirit.

Each and every one of us is intuitive *and* artistic—these faculties are integral parts of our nature, although we may have been led to believe otherwise in the past. We each have a unique expression of creativity that reflects our soul's personality: Some paint, some write, some sing, some cook, some garden, and some do a great load of laundry. The key is to be *artful* as opposed to being an *artist,* much like the difference between being psychic and being *a* psychic. Changing our understanding of these definitions and seeing them as a part of our intuitive language will start us on the path to being artfully intuitive.

We all have an inner art ability (for example, the art of conversation or cooking or letter writing), although it may not be what five-sensory people consider as artistic; just as we all have an inner psychic genius, because we all have a soul, and art and intuition are the wings of our soul. Being "artful," like being psychic, means taking a creative risk. To do so you must leave your head, open your heart, and at times, make a mess—color outside the lines of life and do things spontaneously, whimsically, honestly, and with courage, just as you do when you follow your psychic sense. So the more artful you are, the more intuitive you'll be, and the more intuitive you are, the more artful you'll be, for they support and complement one another.

This reminds me of what happened last year when I went on a ten-city book tour in support of my book *True Balance*. Because being artful is so essential to living the intuitive life, I asked my clairvoyant artist friend, Annette Tacconelli, to come with me to help audiences reactivate their artful expression. At each appearance, she presented a small art project for everyone to try: She passed out index cards and distributed a big pile of crayons on the floor, and then invited each visitor to grab the nearest person and make a drawing with the crayons on an index card together. Many approached the exercise with the same reluctance that they used when trusting their psychic sense, but they were still willing to try. Once they got past their mental roadblocks, they forgot their fear and had fun.

Annette and I faced a very tough audience in Cincinnati—reserved and suspicious, their arms and legs were rigidly crossed, their lips were pursed tight, and they avoided eye contact with each other and us. I told stories and shared my ideas for bringing about balance, including some creative and even silly suggestions, but they didn't laugh at my jokes or try the exercises. I wondered what they were even doing there. But having endured several book tours, I knew better than to let this flatlining response throw me off balance.

However, when I looked at Annette, I could see that she was sweating bullets and feeling seriously challenged. Yet, true to her artful spirit, she leaped up, passed out the index cards, dumped the crayons, and introduced her project with great enthusiasm. No one budged. Undeterred, Annette tried again to encourage the audience to get out of their chairs (and their heads) and have some fun. Still no takers.

A stone-faced woman dryly remarked, "Honey, you're in Cincinnati. In Cincinnati, we don't do crayons." Just then, a child no more than two years of age ran down the aisle heading for the kids' section. With her father following her, she saw the pile of crayons and dove into it, screaming, "Crayons! Look, Dad!

Crayons!" Grabbing them by the handfuls, not believing her good luck, she looked at the deadpan crowd and shouted, "Crayons! Come on, everyone! Let's color!"

The little girl started coloring furiously on one index card after the other. Seeing that no one was moving, she urged them again to join in. This time it worked. One by one, the adults left their chairs, mesmerized by her delight. They grabbed crayons and began to color, and in that moment, the group itself transformed from black-and-white to color. To further fan their initial flame of enthusiasm, we put on some lively African drumming music, and the miracle became full-blown: Cincinnati was coloring! Laughing, moving to the music, exchanging cards, and drawing like mad, their spirits came alive. Once everyone joined in the act, the little girl popped back on her feet, said, "Bye," and ran off as suddenly as she'd appeared.

We spent a few more moments being "artful," as Annette called it, celebrating our creative genius, showing off our brightly colored works of art, and feeling beautifully balanced. Then we shut off the music, put away the crayons, and said good-bye. Our mission was accomplished: The crowd was liberated from the sterile prison of their intellect and rewired to their souls. From the looks on their faces, we knew that they'd had a six-sensory success.

As we were about to leave, no one moved. They'd had so much fun that they didn't want us to go.

One woman shouted from the back row, "Put the music back on—we want to party some more!"

I gently insisted that it was time to go, when the little girl suddenly reappeared and started yanking on my dress hem. "Lady," she said, looking devastated, "the crayons are gone. Where are they?" And in the most desperate, heart-wrenching voice I've ever heard, she said, "I need them!"

Hers was a good question. Where *did* the crayons go? Where did the color and fun go from life? Human beings need art and spontaneity because they feed our soul and inspire our psychic genius. And we six-sensory beings are artists, poets, painters—all creators and inventors in our own way. But being artistic, like being soulful, is not something we do once in a while. It's a way of life for those of us who live in a higher way. Being artful means living life with heart, style, and zest. Like my two-year-old angel, six-sensory people are willing to take risks, make their mark, and turn ordinary moments into extraordinary adventures.

Now take a look at your life. Do *you* allow yourself to have artful moments? Can you let your creative spirit express itself without restriction? It can happen in lots of ways: Visit your local art-supply or crafts store and let your spirit run free. Play with crayons and any other artful medium you desire. What does your psychic genius want to do? Be generous in exploring your creative outlets.

For example, the last time I was in an art-supply store, I saw a little boy of about nine nearly having a fit over all the creative possibilities: Did he want paint? Markers? Chalk? Clay? Tempera? He couldn't decide because he wanted it all. Unfortunately, his mother didn't appreciate his excitement and wanted to contain it. Who knows why? But for whatever reason, it was obvious that she'd long ago backed away from her own free creative expression and had placed her enthusiasm under mental house arrest. "You can't have all of this," she snapped, as he fretted over what he would love most. "Choose one thing," she said, her ego rules squelching his (and her) fun, "and if you're good at it, I'll consider letting you try more. Otherwise it's just a waste."

"That's no fair!" he said. "How can I be good at something if I can't try it first?" (Which made sense to me.)

They continued to argue, and I prayed for the angels to come to the rescue. My vibes told me that the reason this mother was so cranky was because she was jealous. Being controlled by her ego's rules, yet trying to let a little spirit in, she was willing to let her son have a little artful fun, while she was unwilling to let *herself* have any. I had compassion for her and wanted to give her spirit a little boost. When our eyes met, she nodded at me like one condescending mother to another. "These kids," she said, shaking her head. "If I let him, he'd take it all."

"I know what you mean," I said, letting her believe we were

in agreement for a moment. "But if you *did* let him, then there wouldn't be any for you. That's what's not fair. He should get some art tools, and so should you. So what do *you* want to play with?"

Surprised, she wasn't sure how to answer. "I'm not here for me," she said. "I'm no artist."

"Sure you are. Who isn't, really? You just have to be willing to be a bad artist."

She laughed, and her entire spirit opened up, "Well, that I can do."

"I believe you. And doesn't it sound like fun?"

With that thought in mind, she stopped policing her son and went off in search of her own artistic pot of gold. You see, putting your artfulness in action is the same as getting your psychic engines up and running. Each requires that you reach inside yourself, pull out whatever's in your heart, and let it live, breathe, and dance because it's part of you—not because it meets someone else's standards or ideas.

When I ask my clients to do art as a way to their intuition, I inevitably hear their ego recoiling at the idea (because they know it will work): "I can't draw," "I don't paint," or "I'm terrible at art," they say. I tell them not to worry about it. After all, have you ever known a child under the age of four who didn't like to create, speak their truth, or trust their spirit? Probably not, because it's part of who we are and the way we're born. We just get it trained out of us. "I'm not an artist" really means "I'm not someone else's idea of an artist."

If you think about it, that "someone else" probably wasn't much of an intuitive, or much fun either, so let that notion go. Besides, being a "bad artist" really means being a good risk taker, and being a beginner when necessary. It means being faithful to your feelings, inspirations, and heartfelt callings, regardless of what others think or what you've been told.

When I say that you need to be artful to activate your sixth sense and live in your soul, I'm not saying that you should go into the gallery business. I'm suggesting that you start taking more creative time for fun, nonintellectual, artistic pursuits. Everything you do can become art if you want it to and believe it is.

Six-Sensory Practice

This week, visit an art store, a music shop, a dance studio, or some other place where a form of artistic activity has been calling you. Give yourself permission to be a bad artist, and take the risk of enjoying a few creative tools for fun. You don't have to spend a lot of money—a box of crayons and a pad of paper is all it takes. Even a small drum or a kazoo can be exciting with a little effort.

Spend a few minutes every day making bad art: Doodle, color, scribble, dance, make music, and enjoy. If you really want to express your spirit, display your creations in public by posting your work on the refrigerator, dancing in the living room, singing at the table, and appreciating yourself for doing so.

Approach everything you do with an artful flare. As my friend Annette says, "Art is a beautiful voice for your creative and psychic genius." Intuition comes through the heart, most directly through art. And with enough practice, I guarantee that it will start coming through *your soul*, too.

SIX-SENSORY WISDOM:

Be willing to be a bad artist.

SECRET #30

GET INSTANT FEEDBACK

When living a six-sensory life, you'll find it both useful and efficient to have as many tools and techniques for exercising your vibes as possible—so when you're in doubt, must make a choice, or want to find out the truth about someone or a situation, you can do it directly without wasting time thinking about it. One means is to use kinesiology, or muscle testing.

Kinesiology is an established art based on testing muscle response to positive or negative stimuli. A positive stimulus provokes a strong muscle response; a negative stimulus results in a radical weakening of the muscle. Muscle testing can also establish the difference between life-supporting and life-draining situations, and most interesting of all, can discern true from false in any circumstance.

Muscle testing is relatively simple, and if done correctly, foolproof: A strong muscle response means something is supportive, desirable, or true, while a weak muscle response indicates that something is undesirable, or false. The results help you find quick and clean answers and direction without involving the use of your intellect, which can mislead you. The premise behind muscle testing is that your body is part of nature and is energetically connected to the whole, so it can reveal accurate information about the nature of *everything* in the universe, especially when your thinking is kept to a minimum. The body doesn't lie; thus, it can relay accurate feedback about things that affect you.

Kinesiology has been studied by scientists and doctors all over the world and is even used as a diagnostic tool in alternative medicine. A quantum physicist could probably explain why it works so well, but we six-sensory beings don't need to know why it works or how to use it. We use it because it makes intuitive sense to do so, knowing that our body can act as an accurate receiver of information and guides us as a natural part of its job.

When you test accurately, you can get instant psychic guidance on anything at anytime—whether you need a particular vitamin or supplement, whether the used car you want to purchase is a lemon, or whether the vacation destination you have in mind will have good weather during your visit. The options for using muscle testing as a psychic barometer are endless.

The best way to use this technique is the two-person method, in which another person helps you. Thankfully, the assistant needn't be six-sensory, as finding one can sometimes be difficult. (Having said that, for obvious reasons a six-sensory helper is always preferred when dong muscle testing because you'll find that two psychic people are better than one when verifying vibes.) After finding a helper, begin the test to determine if something is true or good for you. First, place your right hand over your belly, and then extend your left arm out to the side and hold it there. Ask your helper to push down quickly on your left wrist while you gently resist. Don't struggle to hold your arm in place—the idea is to find a point of natural resistance and strength against the pressure, which will serve as the baseline for instant feedback. Once established, bring your question or concern to mind in the most neutral way possible without emotion or bias. Don't smile, talk, nod your head, or offer any comments while testing. It also helps to remove metal from your body and have the atmosphere be as quiet as possible.

Let's say that I want to muscle test to discover whether a certain soy-protein product would be beneficial to my health. I'd bring the product to mind as though I were looking at it, but I wouldn't interject my feelings about it—I'd avoid thoughts such as *I love the packaging, I like the flavor,* or *I think it's too expensive,* all of which come from emotion, not intuition. It's better to simply think *soy product.*

Once I have the product in mind, I'd extend my arm to the side and ask my body, "Can I ask this question?" Then I'd ask my helper to press gently down on my arm. If my arm muscles remained strong and resisted the pressure easily, then the answer would be yes, my body agrees to being consulted on this topic. If my arm weakened under pressure and dropped to the side, then my body would reveal my secret resistance to the question and accurately suggest that no, I'm not ready to ask.

If I received a yes, the next step would be to bring the topic to mind and simply say, "Sonia, soy product." Then my helper would press down on my arm again. If the product would energize and support me, my arm muscles would remain strong and resist the pressure easily and remain firmly in place. If the product isn't energizing, my arm muscles wouldn't resist the pressure and would weaken. My arm would fall to my side even though I might want to resist. Of course, I can override this natural weakening and force my arm to remain strong, but not without doing so willfully and with great effort. If that's the case, I'm defeating the purpose of the exercise. If we do this with an open, neutral, and natural mind-set, the body can very accurately counsel us on all matters. For example, I've used muscle testing to select carpeting for our home, to buy a car for our family, and to find a flight to take when traveling.

When I go to the health-food store and see what's available, I tend to get overwhelmed and confused. I've been known to buy all sorts of vitamins and minerals that sound interesting at the time, but most of them end up sitting on the shelf unused. Since discovering muscle testing, however, that's no longer the case. If a product appeals to me, I simply muscle test it to find out whether I need it and if it's right for me. Doing this has simplified the matter of choosing vitamins and remedies significantly for me—I'm now down to a few supplements, and I feel great. I've muscle tested for my kids' vitamins as well. They each tested differently (my older daughter needed more of one thing than my younger one did), so muscle testing helped me customize their supplements as well.

A six-sensory friend of mine used muscle testing to lose weight. With it she discovered that wheat, cheese, and meat weren't good for her system, so she gave them up. On her new diet, she began to slim down instantly and has regained her energy, too. "With muscle testing, my diet nightmare was finally over once and for all," she said, "something that's been a problem for me ever since I was a teenager."

Another six-sensory client uses muscle testing to determine where to place investments. "I figured that my broker was only making educated guesses anyway," she said, "and his suggestions weren't infallible. I don't ignore or disagree with what he suggests—I just muscle test it now. Between the two of us, I feel that I have all my bases covered."

My daughter Sonia, who's going into high school next year, was faced with the task of choosing which school would be best for her. She agonized over her decision for several weeks and finally approached me to muscle test her choices. Once we did, and she came up with a specific school, she was relieved. "That's the school I've been most interested in all along," she told me. "This just confirms my vibes and makes it easier to decide."

I've used muscle testing to help locate people and things, and even used it once to determine if a missing friend was still alive. My brother Anthony contacted me one evening, extremely upset, to say that a mutual friend of ours, Randy, an antique collector and dealer, had gone from his home in Colorado to Detroit to attend an antique show several weeks earlier and hadn't returned when he was scheduled to. He was driving alone, and my brother hadn't heard one word from him in several days.

Because he may have been transporting valuable antiques, Anthony was worried that maybe Randy had been robbed or had an accident and was unconscious and unknown in a hospital. To make matters worse, Randy's father had just died, and Anthony had no one to contact for information. So he came to me for help.

Engaging the assistance of my daughter, we muscle tested for the answers. The results said that Randy was alive, safe, and strangely enough, back home in Colorado. I told Anthony the results and asked to be kept informed. The next morning, my brother called to say that Randy had indeed arrived home safe and sound late the previous evening (just as I'd said). It turns out that our pal had decided to be spontaneous on his way home—he took the scenic route, stopping in small towns along the way looking for treasures, and he didn't think to notify anyone of his delay. Furious at Randy, but greatly relieved, Anthony thanked me for at least one good night's sleep during our buddy's disappearance.

I also use muscle testing for travel decisions, such as asking for hotel guidance, timing, weather information, and even how to pack. Why not? It's practical and extremely accurate, as I found out when I ignored my answers when planning a trip to Albuquerque. My muscle test said to pack for cold weather, although the news said that the city had enjoyed record warm temperatures for the previous ten days. Because it was late March, I believed the newspaper and figured that the good weather would continue, so I packed shorts and T-shirts for all of us.

When we arrived at the Albuquerque airport, it was 75 degrees, but by the time we picked up the rental car, the weather had dropped *30* degrees. By the next morning, it had snowed, so we had to go to a Wal-Mart to get outfitted with sweatshirts, hats, and fleece jackets. Never again would I question what my muscle tests advised, I declared, as I stood there looking like Frosty the Snowman.

My client Georgine had a similar experience with muscle testing versus logic, and thankfully she chose to heed the test results. Georgine had discovered a tiny lump in her left breast, so she went to her doctor for an exam. He ordered a mammogram, but it determined that nothing was wrong. Georgine's muscle test disagreed, suggesting that it was cancerous. She returned to her doctor and pushed for more tests, which he wouldn't approve. He said that she was imagining things and should relax. Georgine couldn't relax, so she changed doctors and got a second opinion. This time she had an ultrasound and a biopsy, which showed that she did have early-stage cancer. She was treated and is now on the mend. I'm not saying that you should muscle test in lieu of a medical diagnosis, but it doesn't hurt to use it as a backup if you're in doubt. Doing so can, as in Georgine's case, shed light on areas that otherwise aren't very clear.

In other words, muscle testing is just another demonstration of your natural six-sensory genius. I have a six-sensory friend, for instance, who muscle tests for which bulbs to plant in his garden, which mechanic to work on his car, and even which client to contact on what day. It doesn't override or take the place of his rational mind—it just takes the place of doubt and insecurity. So if it's not clear, and you're left to guess anyway, why not muscle test? As a six-sensory being, you recognize that doing so is just another way to tap in to the Universal mind for direction, which is what intuitive people love to do most.

The key to accurate muscle testing is to keep your subjective mind out of it. Don't ask your body for its opinion; ask your body for the *truth*. Try it yourself and you'll see what I mean. Someone once told me that real genius lies in making the complex simple. If that's the case, muscle testing is an unbelievably intelligent tool for six-sensory people to use.

Six-Sensory Practice

This week, muscle test everything that interests you. Find your helpers and work together, and don't forget to ask your body, "May I ask this question?" This will eliminate all subconscious resistance and give you a clear channel. Once you get feedback, check it against your vibes: Do they resonate? Does it ring true? Does it *feel* right, even if it isn't what you want to hear? Take your information and use it. And see how much more peaceful you are when you remove doubt.

SIX-SENSORY WISDOM:

Muscle test.

PART IX

The Heart of Six-Sensory Living

SECRET #31

WATER THE AFRICAN VIOLETS

As your sixth sense develops more fully, you'll learn that what propels you past illusion and fear and enables you to live in a higher way is simply love. Love heals old wounds, and it clarifies your vision to help you tune in to what's real and true in others and yourself. Love activates your sixth sense best—when you operate from love, you awaken your Higher Self and express your true self to the world. Love allows you to feel, hear, and understand the hidden world of Spirit with grace, style, and ease.

There are **four basic expressions to your heart center,** but only one opens you to fully function as a creative, intuitive human being:

1. The first is when you love others freely; however, when receiving love in return, you block it and don't take it in. This expression acts as a one-way street, flowing outward in what I call the "chronic exhale mode." People get stuck in this mode because they've been taught that giving love is superior to receiving it, even though this isn't accurate and is, in fact, very damaging to one's spirit. Expressing love in only one way will leave you physically burned out and psychically tuned out. Without enough love, your higher centers of awareness can't open and function properly.

Do you easily give love to others while neglecting your own heart and what it needs? Are you the first to give help but the last to ask for it? If so, then, believe it or not, you're still following ego-based rules. Receiving love without guilt or resistance is basic to balanced psychic living. Spiritual law asks that you accept your vulnerability (your need to be loved) with grace and appreciation—in other words, don't perceive your soul's need for love as a burden, but as simply human.

Receiving love gracefully isn't easy, as I was reminded of several years ago. Even *I* am vulnerable to getting tricked by my ego and must be on constant guard not to fall into its trap. You see, it was my birthday, so my husband and daughters gave me an incredible celebration that began at five in the afternoon. To my surprise, my daughters and I were whisked away in a limousine on a birthday scavenger hunt. And to my utter embarrassment, at every stop along the way one of my friends was waiting with confetti, cookies, and other treats for me. Next, the limo arrived at a beautiful hotel where Patrick was waiting for us. He escorted us to the penthouse, which had a magnificent view of the city, and we were served a private candlelight dinner.

You'd think that this would have been one of the happiest days of my life, but it wasn't. It was almost painful to be showered with so much love and attention, fanfare, and luxury. It scared me to be so appreciated. I know it was only an ego pattern and not my soul feeling this, but it was difficult nonetheless. Instead of enjoying myself, I could hardly wait for it to be over.

I finally leaked out my feelings (my fears) when my kids presented me with their gift. "Stop," I pleaded. "This is too much." And I meant it. My daughter Sabrina got really frustrated. "*You* stop it, Mom," she said. "You always do nice things for us. Let us have a turn, and don't spoil our fun."

When I saw her expression and felt her heart, I understood. It was extremely satisfying and empowering for my family to give me this big surprise. I knew how they felt, as I've enjoyed the same feelings many times in my life. For me to block my family's efforts would have robbed them of joy. So, rather than letting my ego control and block their love, I realized how selfish it would be for me not to accept it. I left my head and jumped right into my heart . . . and loved every minute of the experience that remained.

2. The second expression of the heart is when you accept love freely from others, but you hold your love back and refuse to give it in return. My spiritual teachers said that withholding love is actually a serious form of psychic abuse. Our souls require love just as our bodies require oxygen, and to withhold love is the psychic equivalent of suffocation. When we keep our love from others, we suffocate their spirit. This is an insidious ego-based strategy for remaining in control, and it really does psychic damage.

I'm sure that you've experienced the pain of being with a person with this type of heart. You probably became anxious and struggled to please in order to get his or her heart to open. If the withholding person kept it up, you may have panicked, gotten frantic, and wondered if you're even worthy of love, which is a grave soul injury. The person who kept their feelings locked up may feel temporarily powerful, but the human heart isn't designed to withhold love, so this puts a terrible strain and pressure on it. Locking love away results in stress and heartache that can eventually cause physical damage if done chronically.

Very few conscious soul seekers imagine themselves withholding love, and most are more likely to be "over-givers," if anything. But sometimes we hold back our love in such subtle ways that even *we* are unaware of it. For example, my friend Klaus, who is one of the most aware people I know, told me the following story. He had some beautiful African violets in his office that he loved very much. One day, as he was rushing about, Klaus noticed that the blooms looked a little droopy, and he thought that they needed to be watered. He made a mental note to do so, but it wasn't worth stopping for at that moment. Days flew into each other, and Klaus kept seeing that his violets were drooping badly and seriously needed water. Again, he noted that he needed to water them, and went on about his business.

A few more days whizzed by with no water for the flowers.

At the end of the week, the poor plants had died. Seized with guilt, Klaus realized how he'd chosen to deny them what they needed, and he wondered why he'd done such a thing. He'd known in his heart that the violets needed water, and although he believed he'd get around to it eventually, he never did.

Withholding love, like keeping water from a plant, is death to our spirit. When we disconnect from our hearts, get stuck in our heads, and fall back into following the ego's rules again, our ability to feel and respond to the truth greatly diminishes. Klaus's spirit could see that his flowers were dying, but his heart couldn't feel it. Sadly, it took the loss of his prized plants to open his heart.

Living in a higher way is to realize that love is the most important thing in the world—and it should never be put on hold. A six-sensory being loves first and lets other things follow. Like Klaus, we're all guilty of withholding love without realizing it. We do it when we don't play with our kids, don't walk the dog, or forget to feed the fish or water the plants on time. We do it when we don't take a moment to chat with our neighbor, call our mom, or send condolences to a sick friend. Worst of all, we do it to ourselves when we don't stop to go to the bathroom when we have to, eat when we're hungry, or exercise. We do it when we work tirelessly and never play. We, like African violets, are hearty and can live a long time without what we need. But when we start to die, it's very hard to revive us.

3. The third expression is when we neither give nor receive love; that is, there's no energy exchange on a heart level at all. This is psychically known as being cold- or stone-hearted, and people like this are deeply ill. They've completely succumbed to very harsh ego rules and are in the dark night of the soul. Unfortunately, cold-hearted people are too isolated to receive help directly, but you can send them love to warm their heart at a distance—and you should. We're all connected on a soul level, so when one of us is hurting, we all are. To send love, imagine the other person's heart warming and responding to your energy.

A cold heart occurs when people have been so violated or

injured that they shut down completely. When you're around a cold-hearted person, don't take it personally—and for heaven's sake, don't take it upon yourself to heal this person on your own because you probably won't be able to. Just expect the love you send to do its job, and leave it up to the Universe to do the healing.

A cold heart is difficult to experience, and if you're exposed to such a person, you must be extra loving and compassionate to yourself as well as the bearer. Your psychic battery can get drained very fast, so watch out. Cold-hearted people need patience, and given time and love, their hearts will open.

4. The last expression of the heart is the most joyous. When you give and receive love equally, this clearly reflects living in a higher way. For example, when I was eight, after the frenzy of opening presents on Christmas morning, my younger sister, Soraya (who was two at the time), disappeared into the kitchen after opening her gifts. She was gone for about 15 minutes, returning with presents of her own that she handed out as gleefully as she had opened her own. She gave everyone a piece of toast with butter, wrapped in toilet paper and thread. Hers was as sweet a gift as any I'd ever received, and I envied her giving them. Even then I wondered which was more fun, giving or receiving. As I ate the toast and played with my new Chatty Cathy Doll, I decided that I loved both.

SIX-SENSORY PEOPLE KNOW THAT LOVE is the grease that lubricates the wheels of life. It's the magic elixir that empowers us to operate freely, joyously, and consciously in our surroundings. It transforms the world from a scary, dangerous place into a connected, beautiful stage that's synchronistic and blessed.

If you feel frustrated about not having enough love in your life, you'll be happy to know that it's a self-generating vibration: The more you choose to love, the more love you'll create, and the more love you'll attract. Love yourself and others without hesitation or stinginess, and watch what occurs. Like a magnet, it will draw you to the threshold of more and more love and healing with every expression.

Love is the true foundation of intuitive living—so give it, accept it, inhale it, exhale it, and bask in it. And remember to water the African violets.

Six-Sensory Practice

Practice alternating between giving and receiving love. In the morning, make it your aim to give love immediately and without hesitation wherever you can. Through appreciation, compliments, assistance, patience, and acts of kindness and generosity, love whatever you're invited to love.

In the afternoon, open your heart to *receiving* love—expect and recognize it wherever and however it shows up. If you're given a compliment, accept it and say thank you. If someone asks you if you need anything, say yes and identify it. Practice loving yourself: Take a break, have a nap, or enjoy a few minutes of meditation. Appreciate yourself and say so. List three things an hour that you love about you, and accept and believe them.

Do three loving things for yourself all week. Note how you feel. Is there any difference in your comfort zone between giving and receiving love? If so, strive to narrow the difference, and note, as you do this, how you begin to feel the power of spirit in your life.

SIX-SENSORY WISDOM:

First love yourself, then love your neighbor.

SECRET #32

SHARE

The more we use our sixth sense, the more we'll feel Divine Spirit flowing easily and freely through our lives. We must practice flowing with this generous spirit if we truly want to resonate with the Divine Plan and live in a higher way.

The most immediate way to resonate with Spirit and get in the Universal flow is to give of ourselves rather than remaining fearful and refusing to share. When I began my metaphysical studies with Dr. Tully 32 years ago, one of the first lessons I learned was the law of reciprocity—that is, we get from life what we give to it. If we give support, we'll get support. If we take interest in others, we'll get interest from others. The more we open our heart to share ideas, kindness, enthusiasm, love, and appreciation, the more the same will return to us. It's that simple.

The secret to generosity is to share freely, with no strings attached, no secret agenda, and no unspoken expectations of "now you owe me"—it's the art of giving in a way that's honest and willing, with no thought of return. Giving from the heart, from a place of sharing who you are and what you have with the world, attracts beauty, synchronicity, and harmony to your life. You create balanced relationships with others and begin to establish a gentler, easier, more magical way of living.

I don't think I've met many people who *don't* want to give. Most people want to be generous but may have a hard time doing so because they worry that they don't have enough for themselves, let alone to give to anyone else. Much of this stems from how they were influenced as children. If people were taught the importance of sharing by their parents, then they're usually quite generous, but if they learned to take care of number one first, sharing becomes much more of a challenge. For example, I had a friend who grew up in a large, poor family, where the child who was most generous was most loved. This set up competition between my friend and her siblings, and giving deteriorated into a contest for love, which then led to over-giving and resentment. Not surprisingly, my friend's bigger-than-life efforts where generosity was concerned were attached to an expectation of being loved that could never be satisfied. When I realized that whenever she gave anyone something, she resented it, I told her to stop giving me anything because I couldn't stand the bad vibes that came with it.

Meanwhile, another of my friends expressed a desire to be generous, but she always seemed to focus on taking instead. At lunch, she'd always manage to avoid the check. At potluck-dinner parties, she'd forget to bring something. When we traveled together, she never paid the cab fares or tips. I got so tired of being the sucker that I called her on it. She admitted knowing that she never gave her fair share, but she explained that when she was a young girl, debt collectors would show up on her doorstep to repossess things that her parents couldn't pay for. Consequently, she developed such a fear that her security would be taken away that she couldn't give anything without feeling great anxiety.

Both of my friends followed ego rules that said there was never enough, which made them afraid to give. And that's exactly what they got—not enough. Spiritual law says that there's always enough, and the more you give, the more you'll get. Jesus demonstrated this law with the loaves and fishes: With five fish and two loaves, he fed thousands of people because he just kept giving.

Being unable to give or to be limited in generosity is a psychic wound that arises from either having your basic needs neglected as a child or simply refusing to stop *being* a child. You can heal this psychic injury by focusing on those areas in your life where you can and do give comfortably.

My husband, for instance, came from a large Irish household that struggled to make ends meet, so he has a problem with sharing what's in his wallet. Yet he's the first to make a pot of chicken soup and take it to a sick neighbor, invite our daughter's entire volleyball team over for a pizza party, or bring a bouquet of flowers from his garden to the shut-in down the block. In those areas, he feels abundant and gives with tremendous ease. I also have a client who's tight with a dollar, but he'll show up when someone is moving and carry every last box up and down several flights of stairs. His generosity comes in the form of service with a smile. And I know a woman who hates volunteering—she'll do anything to avoid helping at her kid's school, but she never hesitates to write them a big check. All three of these people are being truly generous where they can be, and that's a beginning.

So identify those areas where you can give without difficulty and go from there. The thing to know is that the more authentically generous you are, the more you link into the eternally abundant web of life. The more you empty your cup to share with others, the more your cup will fill, not just materially, but in every way. The more giving you are, the more you'll activate your psychic sense, because generosity opens the heart, where your sixth sense originates.

Those who are generous in spirit and give fully without holding back are positively charismatic, and they draw things to them like magnets. These are the people who easily share a laugh, give a compliment, take a moment to listen, appreciate those around them fully, and really notice what others do—and they tell them so. This kind of benevolence costs nothing but gives everything. It comes from following spiritual law completely and leaving the rules of the ego behind. Anyone can be generous in this way.

And as you learn to be generous, include yourself. It's not in any Divine Order to give more than you honestly can or want to, or to refuse to receive. When you open your heart, you'll learn that there's no more spiritual merit in giving than in receiving—they're both equal facets of love. So practice being generous, beginning in small ways and gradually expanding. For every decision to give to another, open your heart to receive from others as well. And every time you choose to be generous with another, consider being generous with yourself, too. (As an example, I happily give my teenage daughters rides to their appointments and outings, but I also give myself time to go to the gym or on a bike ride.)

Another measure of balance is to give generously, but not to do more for people than they're willing to do for themselves. For instance, if your friend is in a crisis and calls you for support, listen with compassion, but don't solve her problem for her. She must do it for herself—that's why it's *her* crisis, not yours. If you take on someone else's problem, even in the spirit of generosity, another will simply emerge behind it.

GIVING IS AN ART FORM that elevates your vibration an entire octave. Contributing from an authentic and generous place activates your Higher Awareness and shifts you to being a six-sensory being. It opens the heart and tunes you in to your Higher Self. But the kind of generosity that heals best is to live "full out" rather than being inhibited or restrained in any way (this means no holding back "just in case"). Having faith in reciprocity, unconditional givers generate a thousandfold return. You must be willing to trust that you're an infinite soul who will always have everything you need.

Being generous means taking attention off yourself and focusing on those around you. If you don't feel charitable, the best cure is to practice gratitude. Stop thinking about what's in it for you and see how much is already being given to you. (It can even be helpful to make a list of all that you've been given.) Instead of worrying about what you don't have, think of the Sufi master who, when his house burned down, said, "Good. Now I can appreciate the night stars."

Six-Sensory Practice

Pay attention to ways in which you can give naturally, then do so. Observe how your generosity affects you physically, emotionally, and psychically. And note the areas in which you're not charitable and how that particular energy feels. Practice giving in those areas a little at a time: If you're cheap with money, invite someone to lunch and pay; if you're always rushed, give a loved one a few minutes more of your time; and if you're critical, give others more of your appreciation and affection.

Practice living life fully. Instead of holding back from life, fearing that you'll lose control, dive in headfirst. When you're with people, really *be* with them—help those who help you, listen to those who share their problems with you, and offer others more than you normally do. And begin and end each day by naming at least three things that you're grateful for, striving for new ways to express gratitude each day.

Finally, be generous with *yourself.* Say yes instead of no to things you love, and let in more love, appreciation, and fun each day. Notice how these choices influence your intuition, your creativity, and your sixth sense. Write down all the intuitive gifts that show up this week.

SIX-SENSORY WISDOM:

Be generous.

SECRET #33

SLOW DOWN

One of the great paradoxes of six-sensory living is that in order to accelerate our vibration, we must *slow down*. Conducting our life at a breakneck pace, as we push into the future or obsess on the past, only shuts down our vibes and scrambles our intuitive sensibilities. These behaviors are symptoms of living in our head—we're disconnected from our heart and not trusting the wisdom of the Universe. But by slowing down and focusing on the present, we shift our energy back to our heart, which opens up for inspiration and guidance again.

Sometimes simply stepping away from a situation and allowing a little space is all that's needed. As my teacher Dr. Tully often said, "Sometimes the most powerful thing you can do is nothing." What I've humbly come to understand after experiencing 44 years of intuitive living is that just because we're not doing something doesn't mean that something isn't being done. Something *is* being done behind the scenes in the unseen realm, and we need to make room for it.

Sometimes the mystery ingredient we need to bring backstage action onstage is simply time. The sacred element of timing can save us volumes of wasted adrenaline, not to mention psychic wear and tear. Timing reflects God's wisdom, which works in God's way. When you connect to this Divine pace, you're connected with what I call the "Divine Inhale." It's that sacred pause or quiet space that allows all synchronistic pieces to assemble.

I attended a Chicago Symphony Orchestra concert several years ago, and it was an incredibly beautiful and enriching experience. As the orchestra played the last brilliant phrases of the final work on the program, I held my breath because I was so moved. The last note climaxed in an intense crescendo, like a bolt of lightning crackling through the auditorium, and it left the audience completely silent. The audible music ended, but its energy lingered. It took 15 seconds before its full impact was absorbed—then, like a rush of oxygen, applause broke out and the audience leapt to their feet, wildly cheering the musicians for their extraordinary performance.

Coming home after the concert, I couldn't help but notice that the most powerful moment of the evening for me was the silence. More happened during those 15 seconds than in the entire program. What happened was that I got it: I was able to cellularly absorb not only the performance, but the meaning of it. Had the crowd rushed to applause, I would have missed the heart of the evening. Instead, I got to take the Divine Inhale.

Timing is the Divine's way of again reminding us that we co-create with the Universe—we aren't doing it alone. We plant, water, and weed the seeds of creativity, but we don't have the power to make them grow, let alone grow according to our schedule. How it all unfolds is up to God. God's wisdom will fulfill our deepest intentions once we set them in motion. Our part is to create the perfect conditions for the Universe to flow through us—much like our job is to create the perfect conditions for the garden to grow—but that's all we can do. God flows through us and develops our gardens according to his own timetable. And thank goodness for that, because God knows and grows better than we do.

Because I'm a very energetic and willful person, slowing down has been one my hardest lessons when living in a higher way. I want what I want *now,* and I'll do whatever it takes to create it. Yet I've come to learn that to embrace my dreams I often must just sit and wait. Our soul path unfolds on its own terms, in its own time, and with its own magic.

My client Ellen also learned this lesson when she applied and interviewed for what she perceived to be the ideal job at an Internet company in San Francisco. She felt so certain that she was the perfect choice that she was even willing to quit her present job and move in three weeks (as was required) if she were hired. When she didn't hear from the company immediately, she started calling and campaigning for the job—yet despite her confidence and over-the-edge crusade of persuasion, she didn't get hired.

Ellen was stunned. She'd told everyone that she was getting a new job and moving, so now she faced the embarrassment of admitting her failure. Feeling defeated, she ceased any effort to change jobs and move, and reluctantly began to focus her energies on making herself happier in Chicago. She settled back into her apartment and put her career on the back burner. She spent her newfound free time painting, reading, walking, making friends, and fixing up her home.

Four months later, the dot-com industry collapsed, and the company that had interviewed her disappeared overnight. All Ellen could do was thank God she hadn't been hired and left stranded. Even better, her readjusted ambitions caused her to not only slow down, but to stop climbing the career ladder and get a life outside her job.

WAITING PEACEFULLY AND PATIENTLY for the Universe to work for you is a sign that you're truly starting to move into the spiritual plane. You're intuitively sensing and comprehending the truth that everything is exactly as it should be, moving in exactly the right direction to deliver the best openings and opportunities for your soul's growth. The wisdom of the Universe is bigger, better, smarter, more generous, and infinitely more efficient than you are. By slowing down and backing off, you trust that God is on the job, so you can rest. Slowing down is an act of faith, wisdom, and surrender. And waiting is a show of respect and humility in the face of the Divine forces in the Universe, as they weave your beautiful life together for you and bring it back in their own time as a gift.

When you slow down and allow the open spaces of the unknown to rise up, you will have truly gotten the hang of the six-sensory life. But by then, you won't need me to tell you that—you'll know it in every cell of your body.

Six-Sensory Practice

Give everything a rest. Turn all your plans, dreams, hopes, fears, and ambitions over to God and your guides, and take the week off. Stay off the phone, or keep it to a minimum. And have some fun: Sleep late; see a foreign film; window-shop; go for a long, leisurely walk; or take a bike ride. Rather than fight the river, get in a kayak and ride it! Better yet, let someone else paddle for you. Trust that the Universe will deliver all you need when the timing is right. Don't fret or stress—simply open your heart and wait.

SIX-SENSORY WISDOM:

Relax and enjoy.

And finally,
because you are spirit,
remember to fly!

I hope that by reading this book you've learned that trusting your vibes is an art (an expression of the heart and soul) and not a science (an expression of the ego and intellect), and that, with practice, it will make your life more peaceful and wondrous. Those of us who have mastered six-sensory living will tell you that trusting your vibes is not something to do on occasion if you expect it to work. Rather, it must become a way of life centered on the fundamental intutive practices and based upon the psychic wisdom that I've shared with you in this book.

Trusting your vibes is a way of life that creates a partnership with God and moves you through each day as though it were a dance with the Divine. What you will discover when practicing these six-sensory secrets is that for every step you take toward Divine Spirit by trusting your vibes, it will take a step toward you—and together, you'll create a life of grace, harmony, simplicity, and abundance. This may seem far-fetched and unlikely to the five-sensory person, but to the six-sensory psychic and soulful person, this is only the beginning. It keeps getting better and better.

I invite—even urge—you to join me in the revolution toward six-sensory living. It is the way of the future and necessary if we ever hope to achieve peace and harmony on this planet for all.

┝—◇ ◇ ◇—┥

I would believe only in a God who could dance.
And when I saw my devil I found him
serious, thorough, profound, and solemn
It was the spirit of gravity—through him, all things fall.
Not by wrath does one kill, but by laughter.
Come, let us kill the spirit of gravity
I have learned to walk; since then I have let myself run
I have learned to fly; since then
I do not need to be pushed to move from a spot
Now I am light, now I fly, now I see myself beneath myself
Now God dances through me.

– Friedrich Nietzsche (from *Thus Spoke Zarathustra*)

┝—◇ ◇ ◇—┥

See you in the heavens!
— Sonia

ACKNOWLEDGMENTS

'd like to thank my parents, Sonia and Paul Choquette: You've shown me the wisdom of following my heart and trusting my vibes. I love and appreciate you both.

To my husband, Patrick Tully: Thank you for believing in me and supporting me even when it was difficult to do so—and for allowing me to go so far away and trust that I would return.

To my older sister and best friend, Cuky: Thank you for being my greatest champion and for always believing in me.

To my brother-in-law, Bud: Thank you for always welcoming me and my children into your heart and home without question.

To my dear friends and soul sisters, LuAnn Glatzmaier and Joan Smith: Thank you for holding my hand, charting my course, advising me through life, and being my true soul supporters and friends throughout my journey. Without your direction, encouragement, guidance, and kinship, I'm certain I would have lost my way.

To my freelance content editor, Linda Kahn: Thank you for working so diligently on my behalf, shaping a mountain of papers into a readable manuscript while never once making me feel guilty.

To my freelance copy editor, Bruce Clorfene: Thank you for your lesson in commas and your belief in my work.

To Louise Hay and Reid Tracy at Hay House: Thank you for believing in this project and taking it into the world without hesitation, and especially for providing it with such a wonderful home. I am deeply grateful.

To Jill Kramer, Shannon Littrell, Christy Salinas, Katie Williams, and all the behind-the-scenes people at Hay House who work with such love and dedication to help raise the vibration of this planet: Thank you especially for believing in this project, the most dear to my heart.

To my teachers, Charlie Goodman and Dr. Trenton Tully, who continue to guide me from the Other Side: Thank you for providing me the education and training I needed to fulfill my mission and my heart's desire to serve the world in this lifetime. You were an essential part of my path and, at times, the greatest source of love and comfort for me.

And most of all, to my clients: You have been my greatest teachers over the years. It has been a privilege to serve you, and I humbly thank and honor you all.

)—◇ ◇ ◇—(

ABOUT THE AUTHOR

S onia Choquette is a world-renowned author, story-teller, vibrational healer, and six-sensory spiritual teacher in international demand for her guidance, wisdom, and capacity to heal the soul. She is the author of eight best-selling books, including *Diary of a Psychic*, and numerous audio editions. Sonia was educated at the University of Denver, the Sorbonne in Paris, and holds a Ph.D. in metaphysics from the American Institute of Holistic Theology. She resides with her family in Chicago. Website: **www.soniachoquette.com**

HAY HOUSE TITLES OF RELATED INTEREST

Books

Angel Therapy: *Healing Messages for Every Area of Your Life,*
by Doreen Virtue, Ph.D.

The Body "Knows": *How to Tune In to Your Body and Improve
Your Health,* by Caroline M. Sutherland, Medical Intuitive

Born Knowing: *A Medium's Journey—Accepting and Embracing
My Spiritual Gifts,* by John Holland, with Cindy Pearlman

The Lightworker's Way: *Awakening Your
Spiritual Power to Know and Heal,* by Doreen Virtue, Ph.D.

Meditations, by Sylvia Browne

Miracles, by Stuart Wilde

Power vs. Force: *The Hidden Determinants of Human Behavior,*
by David R. Hawkins, M.D., Ph.D.

Soul Coaching: *28 Days to Discover Your Authentic Self,*
by Denise Linn

The Western Guide to Feng Shui, by Terah Kathryn Collins

You Can Heal Your Life, by Louise L. Hay

Card Decks

The Oracle Tarot, by Lucy Cavendish

Power Thought Cards, by Louise L. Hay

The Prayer of Jabez™ Cards, by Bruce Wilkinson

⊢—◇ ◇ ◇—⊣

All of the above are available at your local bookstore,
or may be ordered by visiting:
Hay House USA: **www.hayhouse.com**
Hay House Australia: **www.hayhouse.com.au**
Hay House UK: **www.hayhouse.co.uk**
Hay House South Africa: **orders@psdprom.co.za**

NOTES

NOTES

NOTES

NOTES

We hope you enjoyed this Hay House book.
If you would like to receive a free catalog featuring additional
Hay House books and products, or if you would like
information about the Hay Foundation, please contact:

Hay House, Inc.
P.O. Box 5100
Carlsbad, CA 92018-5100

(760) 431-7695 or (800) 654-5126
(760) 431-6948 (fax) or (800) 650-5115 (fax)
www.hayhouse.com

———

Published and distributed in Australia by:
Hay House Australia, Ltd. • 18/36 Ralph St.
Alexandria NSW 2015 • *Phone:* 612-9669-4299 •
Fax: 612-9669-4144 • www.hayhouse.com.au

Published and distributed in the United Kingdom by:
Hay House UK, Ltd. • Unit 62, Canalot Studios •
222 Kensal Rd., London W10 5BN • *Phone:* 44-20-8962-1230 •
Fax: 44-020-8962-1239 • www.hayhouse.co.uk

Published and distributed in the Republic of South Africa by:
Hay House SA (Pty), Ltd., P.O. Box 990, Witkoppen 2068 •
Phone/Fax: 2711-7012233 • orders@psdprom.co.za

Distributed in Canada by:
Raincoast • 9050 Shaughnessy St., Vancouver, B.C. V6P 6E5 •
Phone: (604) 323-7100 • *Fax:* (604) 323-2600

———

Sign up via the Hay House USA Website to receive the Hay
House online newsletter and stay informed about what's
going on with your favorite authors. You'll receive bimonthly
announcements about: Discounts and Offers, Special Events,
Product Highlights, Free Excerpts, Giveaways, and more!